RESIDENTIAL SOCIAL WORK
*General Editor:* Tom Douglas

# Residential Group Therapy
# for Children

D0973305

# Residential Group Therapy for Children

*Daphne Lennox*

**TAVISTOCK PUBLICATIONS**

LONDON AND NEW YORK

## Dedication

For my own special 'residential community' – David, Rebecca, Amanda, and Roger, and my mother and father.

First published in 1982 by
Tavistock Publications Ltd
11 New Fetter Lane,
London EC4P 4EE

Published in the USA by
Tavistock Publications
in association with Methuen, Inc.
733 Third Avenue, New York,
NY 10017

© 1982 Daphne Lennox

Typeset by
Scarborough Typesetting Services
and printed in Great Britain by
Richard Clay
(The Chaucer Press) Ltd
Bungay, Suffolk

British Library Cataloguing in
Publication Data

Lennox, Daphne
Residential group therapy for
children.
(Residential social work)
1. Social work with children.
2. Group psychotherapy.
I. Title. II. Series.
616.89'152    RJ505.G7

ISBN 0–422–77550 9

Library of Congress Cataloguing in
Publication Data

Lennox, Daphne.
Residential group therapy for
children.
(Residential social work)
Bibliography: p.
Includes index.
1. Child psychotherapy—Residential
treatment.
2. Group psychotherapy.   I. Title.
II. Series.
[DNLM: 1. Psychotherapy,
Group—In infancy and childhood.
2. Residential treatment—In infancy
and childhood.   3. Social work,
Psychiatric.   WS 350.2 L568r]
RJ504.5.L464 1982   618.92'89152
82–8187

ISBN 0–422–77550–9 (pbk.)

# Contents

# Acknowledgements

It would be impossible to name all the people who have taught and influenced me, through precept and example, about the exciting challenges, the pains and pleasures of residential social work and special education, which I have tried to share with fellow practitioners in this book. I would like to thank all my 'teachers', past, present, and future and especially all the children with whom I have worked who have been my most important mentors.

I particularly acknowledge the support and encouragement of my husband, David, with whom I have shared all the heartaches and fun of our joint careers in residential work with children, and my special friends, the staff and children of Highfield School. In particular, I am grateful to Elsie Davenport for reading my script.

Tom Douglas will, I trust, take it as the compliment I mean it to be when I thank him for being my father figure! His advice and encouragement have been invaluable.

Above all, I wish to thank Mona Hill, who has, with infinite patience, perfectionism, and friendship, typed my manuscript.

I have always been grateful for the imaginative support for my work at Highfield given to me by my Education Authority and Board of Governors but would stress that the ideas expressed in this book are my own and do not necessarily reflect those of my employing authority.

# General Editor's Foreword

The original impetus to create a series of books on residential work came from the realization that although there were very many residential institutions, very little attempt had ever been made either by residential practitioners or others to commit to writing the practice wisdom which the profession undoubtedly possesses. No one can spend a large number of the days of his or her life for several years in the kind of close contact that a residential situation produces, without having learned some effective methods of handling the more common problems such an existence entails.

Not all such experience-based practice is necessarily good, but as long as it was successful in the particular institution in which it was used, in helping the residents in that institution achieve their agreed goals, then it is worth at least a look. Why did it come about? How successful was it? Why was it successful? Other similar questions must be asked and the answers recorded for all those interested to see. If this is not done, then whenever similar problems arise they will each have to be dealt with as if the problem were occurring for the first time. Much time and effort are wasted in this way and many residents get a worse service than if the information on practice were available.

As Daphne Lennox says in her introduction, she has been in the residential care business for twenty-five years, and what comes across in this text is a strong sense that having garnered experience for this period of time she wants to present it to others, to shorten their search for suitable approaches for use with their own residents. No doubt many have written more fully about the approaches of transactional analysis, behaviourist, and encounter groups which she outlines here. But what is important is that Mrs Lennox can write about these approaches not just as theoretical concepts, but as practical techniques tried in her own residential community. The warts and the blemishes of the methods are far more interesting to those who would want to try and use them, than the smooth sense of abstraction which theory often gives.

In a word Mrs Lennox has found a role which is of paramount importance in any professional field, that of translator. She is able to effect a bridge in good straightforward terms, a link, between the concept of the theoretician and the principles and techniques of the practitioner, a link which can only be forged by those with a goodly amount of experience of both ends of the continuum.

Too often, little-enough use is made of the time residents spend in an institution other than for the purposes of maintenance and containment. If residents are to be offered the chance of change, then residential institutions offer an enormous advantage in the intensity of contact available. No therapist working in weekly sessions, no field worker is presented with such an effective method of counterbalancing other environmental effects as is the residential worker.

Sadly however this advantage is often wasted because residential workers don't know how to use it or their accepted methods of working take little cognizance of it. There is often the hope, frequently offered by group workers in other spheres, that the mere fact of putting people together will effect some form of change in their behaviour. Indisputably it will. But it may be a reinforcement of all those behaviours which have previously created problems.

This text offers positive suggestions for ways to tackle problems presented to a residential community by the children in it. Millham *et al.* (1981:10) suggested that there was evidence to show that staff and boys in some residential institutions 'had different perspectives on what residential experience is about' which tended to vitiate any attempts to change behaviour. This lack of fit in the perceptions of the protagonists in residential treatment can only be reduced by a thorough assessment of expectations coupled to a high level of understanding on the part of the residential staff. This element of clarity, of transparency, is an essential part of the approaches detailed here.

Even in the apparent confusion of the 'real' situation, Mrs Lennox' text should lead to an enhanced element of precision in what the practitioner does — and however small that element may be, it will still be pure gain both to practitioner and resident.

TOM DOUGLAS
*February 1982*

# Preface

Looking back over my twenty-five years' experience in residential social work and residential special education, I realize that my personal development as a practising therapist has been in the nature of a search for the Holy Grail of a 'perfect therapeutic technique'.

From the total blind confidence of youth, when I was absolutely sure that I had all the rights answers, to my present position of knowing that the more one knows the more there is to know, it is possible to trace the varying trends in the psychology and philosophy of therapy which have played a significant role in my professional development.

It is the techniques arising from three of the major theoretical approaches to therapy and the way in which they can be incorporated into a therapeutic community which I would like to share, in this book, with fellow practitioners.

I understand only too well the difficulties of applying oneself to keeping up to date with theory when one is often totally absorbed and sometimes exhausted from practice, so, with this in mind, my aim is to present what I consider to be useful theoretical background in as simple a form as possible.

Each theoretical exposition will be followed by suggestions for its practical application in a residential setting in the hope that, when the reader has reached that head-scratching point of saying, 'Whatever shall I try now with the group?', he may turn to this book and find a little inspiration.

# 1   The Therapeutic Group Milieu

Before embarking on a detailed examination of three different approaches to group therapy, I would like to look at the total group therapy potential of the residential community for children.

Living and working in a residential setting we are inevitably involved in a gigantic and continuous 'group experience'. This is true of a group of students living together in a hall of residence or of sailors living aboard ship.

What distinguishes the 'group experience' of staff and children living together in a residential community is that the primary task of the group is the creation of a cohesive group which will enable its members to grow and develop into happy, fulfilled, and adequately socialized members of the various other groups – home, school, society – in which they have to survive.

At its best a residential community will facilitate this development for each member, including members of staff who do not stand outside the group experience but are essentially part of it. One hopes that the difference between the staff and children participating in the group will lie, not so much in what each is able to take from the group, but in what each is able to bring. It is safe to assume that a very high percentage of children who find themselves living in a residential community will bring very personal and pressing problems with them as a result of previous poor experiences. Staff, one hopes, will bring the minimum of personal problems into the group and the maximum of constructive attitudes and helping techniques.

If each member of staff is to make the fullest use of his personal qualities and repertoire of techniques, it is vital that he seeks to understand, not only the needs of each individual child, but also the forces at work within the group itself. What are the most important of these forces and how do they affect residential social workers and the children with whom they live and work? Many writers on group work have compiled their own list of basic assumptions about groups. Douglas (1976:28) for instance, outlines eight basic assumptions:

'(1) that group experience is universal and an essential part of human existence

(2) that groups can be used to effect changes in the attitudes and behaviours of individuals

(3) that groups provide experiences which can be monitored or selected in some way for beneficial ends . . .

(4) that groups offer experience shared with others so that all can come to have something in common with the sense of belonging and of growing together

(5) that groups produce change which is more permanent than can be achieved by other methods and change which is obtained more quickly also

(6) that groups assist in the removal or diminution of difficulties created by previous exposure to the process of learning

(7) that groups as instruments of helping others may be economical in the use of scarce resources, e.g. skilled workers, time, etc.

(8) that a group can examine its own behaviour and in so doing learn about the general pattern of group behaviour (process).'

Other experienced group workers, e.g. Thompson and Kahn (1970:10–28) have stressed, in addition to the constructive forces at work in a group, the existence of potentially destructive elements in any group. They have observed the competing needs and drives in individuals being mirrored at group level and view the simultaneous existence of cohesive and disruptive forces in a group as one of the basic assumptions about groups which the aspiring group worker must take into account. If we accept that working with children in a residential setting is, in itself, a form of group work, it becomes obvious that it is essential to understand the nature of the positive and negative forces at work in our particular group.

Most of the assumptions made about groups of adults are equally applicable to groups of children in a residential community but there is one important additional factor to take into consideration. Adults in group therapy usually have the power to withdraw from the group if they feel unbearably threatened by what is happening to them or that their individual needs are not being met. Children in a residential community do not usually have such autonomy. It is therefore very important that the powerful adults in a children's community learn to understand what is happening to each child, both as an individual and as a member of the group, and that the adults learn to treat, with respect and responsibility, their ability and skill to manipulate and utilize group processes constructively or destructively.

When we walk, for the first time, into a residential community for children, it is possible to sense within minutes the quality of life in that community. Our antennae are picking up the thousand and one tiny clues to the existence of benevolent and malevolent forces at work and we feel capable of making a rapid judgement about the warmth, or lack of warmth, in the community, the degree of acceptance for individuals, the existence or non-existence of authority and control. We are making an intuitive assessment of the group dynamics at work within that particular establishment. Children coming to live in the community will make a similar rapid judgement which may affect, profoundly, the degree to which they will trust themselves to the group and will certainly influence their expectations of help. Therefore, before we as staff employ our skills to design individual and group therapy programmes for the children, it is essential that we create an overall ambience which will encourage the potentially constructive forces within the group to dominate the potentially destructive forces.

This brings us to an examination of the residential group as a therapeutic milieu or therapeutic community in which more specialized individual and group therapies can be employed. There have been many descriptions and definitions of therapeutic communities and a comprehensive evaluation of underlying theories and progress has been attempted in Hinshelwood and Manning (1979). The major theme in this book is that the concept of the therapeutic community is now widely accepted and that the pioneering spirit of the early communities is at present being replaced by a movement towards standardization creating a tension between the need for innovation and the need for routine. If we are to preserve a healthy dynamism in our residential community and combat complacency and resistance to change we must be prepared to involve ourselves in a continuous evaluation and reappraisal of the tenets we believe to be at the foundation of our structure.

I would like to isolate some of the most important underlying principles of a therapeutic milieu and discuss them under the following headings:

(1) acceptance and empathy;
(2) the value system;
(3) the physical environment;
(4) task definition;
(5) role definition and communication.

### ACCEPTANCE AND EMPATHY

Acceptance and empathy are much-used words in social work and special education but are concepts which it is much easier to absorb theoretically than to put into practice. I believe that the cornerstone of effective therapeutic groups is acceptance, in the sense of unconditional respect for the individual, as he is. However, it is when we attempt, or are asked, to give unconditional acceptance for any behaviour whatsoever displayed by children that we come up against difficulties. Each child living in a residential community has a right to some protection from the more damaging aspects of another child's behaviour and we, as the caring adults, have an obligation to provide this. Achieving a balance of genuine respect and empathy for the feelings and behaviours of individuals whilst providing adequate protection for the rights of all members of the group is the first major challenge for the residential group worker. The more each child and member of staff is enabled to understand other group members' needs as well as his own, the more this balance is likely to be achieved.

Some communities achieve this mutual understanding through daily or regular group discussions, some through more intense individual discussion, but one of the most powerful methods of helping a child towards acceptance of and empathy for others is through modelling. A more detailed discussion of the principle of 'modelling' in the behaviourist sense of the word will follow in Chapter 4 but here it is relevant to examine its general influence in the creation of a therapeutic milieu.

While lunching recently at a residential community for children in care a member of staff expressed concern to me about the rigid pecking order we could see at each children's table. The strongest child at each table was served first and had the most food, the least influential child practically starved. What was interesting was that I was sitting at the staff table where an equally rigid hierarchy was observable. The head-teacher was always served first and the status of each staff member was obvious from the order of serving.

The children's culture in a community invariably mirrors that of the adults and the ability of staff to show empathy and acceptance for each other will be a significant model for the children. The tone and manner of voice we use to each other in the staff group, the degree of tolerance for each other's idio-syncracies and foibles and the respect and humour with which we relate to each other will all affect the way children relate to us and to each other. If there is a healthy and dynamic inter-acion in the staff group there is much more likely to be a similar interaction in the children's group.

Therapists from approaches as varied as Freud's psycho-analysis, Carl Rogers' client-centred approach, and Wolpe's behaviourist approach have all emphasized the importance of warmth and empathy in the therapeutic relationship. Freud (1912:319) spoke of the curative effects of 'warmth or positive affect'. Rogers stresses again and again in his work the role of non-possessive and unconditional warmth (1951, 1961, 1970) and respect for the client as he is. Whereas behaviour therapists would approach the question of therapy by observation of behaviour and not of feeling, they nevertheless still emphasize the importance of acceptance and warmth. Wolpe, for example, (1958:106) states:

'All that the patient says is accepted without question or criticism. He is given the feeling that the therapist is unreservedly at his side. This happens not because the therapist is expressly trying to appear sympathetic, but as a natural outcome of a non-moralizing objective approach to the behaviour of human organisms.'

How realistic is it for us, as residential social group workers, to display this unconditional warmth when much of the behaviour of our client children is frankly totally unacceptable to the other members of the community? Should there not come a moment when, as part of the therapy, it becomes right to put in some social and behavioural demands from a child and to make our acceptance conditional at this point? Happily most babies who come into the world are met initially with unconditional acceptance and love from their parents in spite of their anti-social behaviours, such as keeping the whole household awake at night!

Many of the children who come into residential communities, however, have never experienced this period of unconditional acceptance from their parents and will look to their new 'home' to provide this. If the staff are able to accept each new child with a genuine respect for him as an individual and to put in, initially, as few conditions for approval as possible, this will provide an overall climate of warmth and tolerance which other children, looking back to their own entry to the community, will be able to understand and tolerate even though they, by now, may have reached a stage in treatment where more is expected from them. It is often said by and to residential workers that it is important to treat all children equally, otherwise we will reinforce their feelings of life having treated them unfairly. Real equality for children in a residential setting is indeed important but does not necessarily lie in each child's receiving exactly the same treatment. Children will accept differing degrees of conditional and unconditional acceptance if they are helped to feel that they are being treated equally in that their individual needs, though different from some of their peers' needs, are met with equal respect and thoughtful planning.

If this respect for individual need is genuinely present in a residential community the new child entering the community will sense this immediately and will usually start to trust that the caring adults on the staff are firmly on his side. Not all children, however, will wish to be accepted with an effusive show of physical affection. Storr (1960) talks of a continuum of personality types ranging from the schizoid personality at one end of the continuum to the manic-depressive personality at the other extreme of the continuum. He maintains that to the person who is nearer the schizoid type the biggest threat to security lies in other people getting so close that his own personality or ego will be overpowered and perhaps annihilated, whereas to the person approaching the manic-depressive end of the continuum the biggest threat to security lies in fears of rejection when other people are not close enough. If we are to show our acceptance of and empathy for a new child in a sensitive manner, it is important that we make a rapid assessment as to whether a new child feels the need of immediate close physical contact or wishes to remain physically aloof until he feels secure.

Acceptance and empathy therefore come to mean, not an unconditional acceptance for every piece of behaviour, however anti-social, but unconditional respect for each person as an individual and a skilled and sympathetic approach to the needs of each child, be they for a period of unconditional approval and physical closeness or the provision of consistent caring control at a physically safe distance.

One last point I would like to make from my own experience and observation of staff is that however qualified and experienced we are in our profession we can rarely experience the totally unconditional acceptance for other people's children that we feel, at a primitive animal level, for our own child. Social workers, both in residential care and in the field, have often been accused of claiming to be omnipotent and omniscient and we are in danger of living up to this criticism if we maintain that we can show, to every child who crosses our path, total empathy and total acceptance. I am making this point because I have seen staff display such strong guilt when they have less than god-like feelings towards certain children that they are unable to draw on the professional skills which they do possess. As Winnicott (1965:57) said when talking about mothering, realistically there is no such person as a perfect mother — what we should aim to be is a 'good enough' mother. In a residential community we are aiming to show 'good enough' empathy and acceptance for each child and in order to do this we should be prepared to try and understand life from the child's point of view before planning our treatment strategy. If '*tout comprendre c'est tout pardonner*' is true, our capacity to show genuine respect and acceptance for each child will grow as we learn to understand more.

## THE VALUE SYSTEM

Assuming that the new child has made a rapid intuitive assessment that the level of respect and tolerance for him and his problems is acceptable in this home and that he can safely trust himself to his environment and look to it for support and security, his next task will be to seek to understand the value system of the community. At its simplest level this will mean finding out what is allowed and what is forbidden — what is rewarded and what is punished. I have found that it is more effective initially to encourage existing child members of the community to undertake this initiation process than to rely on staff explanations which may still be mistrusted by a child who does not yet know the adults concerned.

Communities vary in the number of explicit rules within which they function and rules may be arrived at in a variety of ways. In some establishments rules are made simply by the staff or even solely by the head but most therapeutic communities aim at a high degree of client involvement in the creation of rules. Some communities not only arrive at the rules through a democratic process but also make the whole group responsible for meting out punishment.

Whatever the methods used by a group to arrive at a workable structure for the life of the community, what will really come over to the children is the true value system which underpins the overt rules. To give a simple example, I have heard staff say to a new boy or girl being introduced to the rules, 'We'll have no bloody swearing here!' Smoking, which often poses a problem in a residential community, is hard to criticize in children if most of the staff around them are regular smokers. The attitudes and behaviours which are genuinely unacceptable to the ruling adults will be observable in the way children comment on each other's behaviour as well as through observation of the direct interventions by staff. Children are also very astute at picking up the real relationships between members of staff and if negative criticism, sarcasm, and intolerance of different points of view are rife in the staff group no amount of rule-making will eliminate those attitudes in the children's group. Similarly, the traits, attitudes, and behaviours which are really valued, first by the leader and subsequently by the staff, and consequently rewarded by approval in the form of praise, encouragement, and warmth will tend to be mirrored in the children's group and quickly evaluated by a new child.

Much of the value system of a residential community is implicit rather than explicit but in order to ensure that the system is appropriate to the task it is important that staff and children are as consciously aware of the norms which govern their community life as is possible. Napier and Gershenfeld (1973:82–4) have classified group norms under four headings.

## (1) Formal norms

These are the norms which are imposed by the governing body of the community and may or may not be written down. These norms, e.g. that in a school regular teaching sessions will form a part of each weekday, will mark the parameters within which the group can function.

## (2) Explicit norms

Some norms are explicitly stated as rules of the house and passed on verbally to new members of the group but may not necessarily be the actual norms, e.g. we have no barriers here between staff and children — but the children are not allowed into the staff room!

### (3) Non-explicit, informal norms

Most residential groups develop a set of informal norms which rapidly become traditions though never having been stated as norms, e.g. in my particular residential community morning coffee is taken by staff in the relative peace of the staff room but lunch and afternoon breaks tend to be taken in the central staff/children sitting area.

### (4) Unconscious norms

These are often in the nature of taboos. In a mixed residential setting they are frequently to do with sex, e.g. male members of staff will not be expected to demonstrate the uninhibited show of physical affection for boys or girls in the way that female staff will be encouraged to do.

Once the child has made an assessment, however unconsciously, of the general value system, he will start to explore the ways in which these values affect him as an individual. Most therapeutic communities will pay lip service to the principle that it is important to involve the child in his own treatment programming but in practice this varies from a detailed 'contract' approach, where each stage of what is going to happen to the child is discussed and agreed with him, to a very loose 'we've talked it over with him' approach. Not only will the child look for a show of respect for his future from his members of staff but also for a show of respect for his past. Children entering a residential therapeutic community rarely come 'trailing clouds of glory' but frequently come trailing clouds of misery. Some staff are wary of reading a child's file before getting to know him as they feel that their spontaneity will be in some way jeopardized and their opinions prejudiced if they know too much. However, if one is to approach a child with sensitivity and true empathy for his problems it is far better to know as many of the facts about his life as possible in order to relate to him with understanding.

Linked with his need for understanding of his personal life will be a need for understanding of his previous cultural norms. A residential community often takes children from a wide range of social backgrounds and expects them all to conform, often rapidly, to a totally alien culture. If our cultural norms concerning table manners, modes of speech and dress are too inflexible to incorporate happily a wide range of previous norms we are going to make many children feel alien to their new environment. Redl and Wineman (1952:59), talking of their own therapeutic community, stress the importance not only of 'guaranteed symptom tolerance' but also of 'old satisfaction channels' being respected. It is not enough within our value system to respect the child himself, we must also convey to him our respect for what he has been as well as for what he can become. Amongst the old satisfaction channels a child brings with him there will be a relationship with at least one close family member which he will wish and need to maintain. It is easy for staff in a residential community, dealing with the child in isolation from the family, to ignore or undervalue this need – especially if the family has been assessed as totally inadequate or downright destructive to the child. If we are truly seeking to encourage feelings of self-worth and value in each child, we cannot ignore the fact that most children, however ambivalent their own feelings for their parents, will wish us to show respect for their mother and father as a mark of respect for they themselves.

THE PHYSICAL ENVIRONMENT

Perhaps it would have been more appropriate to discuss the importance of the physical environment before discussing the psychological environment that meets a new child on entering a residential community as it is the building and the approach to the building which create the first impression. I have chosen, however, to put it second in importance as I have visited several highly successful therapeutic communities which were housed in far from ideal premises and vice versa. Nevertheless the physical environment and the way it is used symbolize the value system of a community.

Madge (1951) maintains that 'buildings should symbolize mother's body – with the lawns and garden outside as socio-physical space into which our libido flows to encounter the world'. Perhaps this is a little too poetic to apply to many of our residential communities but most buildings, however austere superficially, can be adapted, with warmth and imagination on the part of the inhabitants, to convey this womb-like security. When Maxwell Jones was commissioned by the Prison Service in 1950 to suggest ways of raising inmate morale he concluded that there was a significant relationship between group morale and the physical environment. In *The Therapeutic Community* (1953) Jones maintains that rooms have behavioural expectations – soft furnishings ease tension and communicate 'we care for you' in the same way that hard, plain, uniform cold surfaces symbolize rejection and evoke apathetic or even violent behaviour.

There is something about the arrangement of furniture in a building as well as the type of furniture and decoration which conveys an abundance, or lack, of warmth and welcome. Fritz Redl (1952:42) talks of 'A House that smiles, Props which invite, Space which allows'. On coming into a therapeutic community, children will immediately be able to assess whether toys and books are freely available or not, whether bedrooms are places of comfort and retreat or places for impersonal use or even punishment, and whether the furniture and 'props' are strictly one-purpose designed or have possibilities for fun and imaginative play. Most children will find endless simple pleasure, for example, in making dens under stairs or in corners and permission to move furniture about and to add or subtract it from a room gives scope for fantasy games of spaceships, submarines, and enchanted woods. The opportunity for thera-peutic role play is dependent not only on sensitive staff partici-pation but also on 'Props which invite' and 'Space which allows'.

Traditionally in institutions colour schemes and furnishings were picked for their practicality in terms of hard wear, furniture was arranged, often round the four walls of a room, to facilitate easy cleaning. Although this is still apparent in some old people's homes, mental institutions, and day rooms in hospitals the majority of residential communities for children are now happily designed on a more 'homely' pattern. Steiner, in his work with maladjusted children, pioneered the therapeutic use of certain colour schemes and room shapes and has influenced the design of many residential communities. The Churchill Hospital in Oxford, for instance, used the Steiner-like model of a classroom as a safe, holding environment and constructed in the hospital grounds a number of 'womb-like' dwellings to be used for the regressive treatment of disturbed children. Not all residential communities, however, are purpose-built and some of those which are prompt the question, 'To what purpose?' but most buildings can, with adaptation and imagination be geared to the needs of the children and staff and the purpose of the community.

When deciding on the major environmental needs a child will experience on coming into a residential community, it is worth considering our own reactions when going to stay in a new environment − perhaps a hotel on holiday or a friend's house. First, we will want to know where we are going to sleep and where we can safely leave our personal possessions. We will soon view this as our own private territory within the building and we will expect it to offer some privacy and safety from invasion. Most residential communities for children will not be able to offer each child his own bedroom but if staff have a genuine respect for a child's territorial rights it is usually possible to create at least a small space around a bed which the child can think of as his own and which staff and other children will not enter without permission. I remember one small Liverpool boy, who was showing me the dormitory of the children's home where he lived, pacing out an area of about ten square feet around his own bed and saying, 'Everything inside that is Liverpool − and you'd better ask before you come in!' I think it is one of the saddest comments on residential social work when one is shown a bedroom or bed-space in a community and it is so impersonal that it is impossible to guess whether it belongs to a young or older child or even to a boy or girl.

The second area we are likely to be interested in is where we can eat. The kitchen and dining room are often the heart of a community and the messages they convey in terms of accessibility and enjoyment of food will be similiar to ours when we take our first meal in our hotel. Communities vary in the degree to which they allow children to participate in the preparation and serving of meals and the formality or informality in which meals are taken.

Again, if we are prepared to use our own criteria for the enjoyment of a meal many of the institutional mores surrounding meal times will seem redundant. Why we should expect children to eat in large groups at a table when small groups are much more conducive to friendly conversation, and why we should present food in unattractive, utilitarian dishes, is a mystery. The physical arrangement of the dining room, as of the bedrooms, can be subtly manipulated to help each child to feel important and valued as an individual.

Other areas of importance in the building will include warm and private bathrooms and toilets where a child can feel safe from staff or peer group intrusion. I have known children in some communities develop a phobia about bathing simply because they are unable to lock the door and therefore fear intrusion.

Osmond (1957:23) described small areas where the furniture is arranged to encourage small groups to meet and the members to interact freely as 'socio-petal' areas. Whereas most residential communities will have an area large enough for the whole group to meet together − an essential feature of a building − not all will have sufficient of these socio-petal areas to allow small groups of children, staff, or a mixture of both to meet in comfort and relative privacy. Sometimes it is possible, with a little imagination and ingenuity, to create these areas out of unused spaces in stair wells or spare corners of the building. Sometimes a corner of a large room can be adapted.

Having stressed the importance of providing some spaces for privacy and some for the intimacy of small groups I think it is also important that some parts of the building and the grounds should provide an area where a child can feel relatively anonymous. Living in a residential community can be, for staff and children alike, somewhat like living in a goldfish bowl and it can be a relief to a child to know that there is at least one place where he can relax or let off steam and not be too directly under the eye of staff.

One of the problems connected with the exploitation of the physical environment of a residential community is the need for staff supervision of children. Should children be under the protective or critical eye of staff at all times and therefore banned, for example, from using bedrooms except at bedtime? Should rooms which contain valuable property be locked to avoid the temptation to steal, experienced by many children in institutions? If children are not supervised constantly, will they indulge in undesirable sex activities or smoke and set the building on fire? These, and similar problems, arise perennially in residential communities and the solutions we decide upon will influence not only the philosophy of the community but also the manipulation of the physical environment.

Some of the factors which govern the way we decide to use the physical environment are to do with external pressures on the staff in the form of expectations from governors, administrators, and visiting councillors. Although people in these roles may genuinely support the philosophy of a community which aims to help children to feel secure and 'at home', they may, at the same time, expect to find in the building a standard of tidiness, cleanliness, and order which would far exceed that in the homes from which the children have come or that of any average home. In an age when increasing cuts in expenditure are taking place it is often difficult to replace furniture or redecorate rooms and it becomes a very real problem for staff to decide whether to let a child move and play with furniture and risk its being damaged or to decorate his own 'territory' in a way which may not meet with approval from inspecting adults.

There are no easy answers to these problems and the rules governing the use of the physical environment in a residential community will be determined to a certain extent by the group leader's ability to present the task of the community clearly and convincingly, not only to the staff, but also to the external governing body so that the integration of task and environment can be achieved.


## TASK DEFINITION

If we are to succeed in integrating task and environment in a therapeutic community it is essential that we have a clear definition of the overall task of the establishment and of the specific tasks of each member of the community. It is not enough to say that the organization exists to provide therapy. This gives no clear guidelines to staff. It is too generalized and is open to differing interpretations which may conflict and hence become counter-productive. Hey (1973:7) maintains that 'tasks can be described as pieces of work with specific intended results which the worker expects himself, or is expected by others, to attain within some explicit or implicit time-scale. That is, he is expected to produce results and he has not got forever to do so.' The idea that there is a time-scale to therapy is anathema to some residential workers especially if their therapeutic goals for the children are unrealistic in the first place and therefore unlikely to be achieved. In a field where resources are strictly limited in terms of money and personnel it is important that we use our scarce resources to their best advantage and do not waste too much energy on 'lost causes'. It may be argued that by definition any child who finishes up in a residential community is already a 'losing cause' but, in order to do the job, we have to believe that our intervention in the child's life has the potential to reverse the downward slide for him. What I am terming a 'lost cause' therefore is not the child himself but any unrealistic aims which members of staff, often in collusion with parents, have set for the child. How often do members of staff with a high degree of care and concern for a particular child make statements like, 'If we can just get his parents to be happy with each other and get grandmother out of the way and explain to them how they should relate to Johnny, etc., everything would be all right'? No doubt! The reality, however, is more likely to be that parents will get divorced, that grandmother will continue to interfere unhelpfully and that there will always be some misunderstanding in the relationship between Johnny and his parents.

If this sounds totally cynical and discouraging to residential workers it is not meant to do so. By insisting on the definition of the task being realistic I am anxious to prevent the disillusionment and bitterness often felt by staff when they fail to achieve their own goals. Rice (1958:99), in his study of productivity and social organizations, isolates three main characteristics of realistic and satisfactory tasks:

'(1) A task should be so organized that it is a 'whole' task.
 (2) Those engaged on the task should be able to control their own activities.
 (3) Tasks should be so organized that people can form satisfactory relationships.'

It is possible to provide 'whole' tasks for staff in a therapeutic community if the major task of rehabilitating the child is broken down into small, achievable, and progressive units which will provide satisfaction and a sense of achievement for staff and child alike. The staff in my own residential community complete a weekly goal sheet for each child under the following headings:

(1) Relationships
 (a) with houseparent
 (b) with teacher
 (c) with peers
 (d) with other adults
(2) Behavioural Changes
(3) Interaction with home and any other outside agencies.

Teachers include specific educational goals for the week and each objective is discussed with the child and anyone else involved. At the end of each week the degree of success in achieving each goal is rated with the help of the child, on a 0–4 scale, and a decision is made about whether to modify each particular goal, or continue with, or perhaps abandon it for the time being. If the goals set and tasks defined are well within the capacity of staff and child, senior staff can then feel quite confident to subscribe to Rice's second point that 'those engaged on the task should be able to control their own activities'.

His third point, that 'tasks should be so organized that people can form satisfactory relationships', is highly pertinent to residential communities. Satisfactory relationships are not just desirable in a residential community, they are essential tools of the trade. We have already seen that the way in which the staff relate to each other will influence the way in which they relate to children and children relate to each other. In order to keep these relationships satisfactory we must work hard at minimizing frustration which can often occur when we ourselves, or our colleagues, are not clear what it is we are trying to do or have been set impossible tasks.

It is important, therefore, that the overall primary task of the unit is understood and discussed by all and that specific tasks of each member are equally understood by all. By 'all' I would include not only staff and child but also parents and any other outside agencies who impinge on the child's treatment. Some therapeutic communities use written contracts to be signed by the child and his parents before the therapy begins. These seem particularly effective when used with older children who are able to conceptualize their problems to some degree and are capable of understanding the vocabulary employed. Very young children may not be able to verbalize their anxieties or enter into an explicit contract for their therapy but can be helped to understand themselves more through play, role-play, and non-verbal communication. Whatever method of task definition is used it should be a continuous process and staff concerned in defining tasks should be prepared to take into account the changing needs of the individual child, the group, and the community as a whole.

As Rice (1958:33) concluded in his analysis of a successful organization in terms of output:

'The performance of the primary task is supported by powerful social and psychological forces which ensure that a considerable capacity for co-operation is evoked among the members of the organization created to perform it. As a direct corollary, the effective performance of a primary task can provide an important source of satisfaction for those engaged upon it.'

## ROLE DEFINITION AND COMMUNICATION

Whatever a person's occupation or life-style, he will be called upon to play several different roles at different parts of the day or at different stages of life; for example, husband, father, son, grandfather, breadwinner. In most occupations it is relatively simple to define the particular role one is playing at a given moment and to differentiate between roles which are often specific to a particular setting, e.g. home, place of work, place of play. In a residential community which is both home and place of work for all resident staff and children this definition and differentiation is not always as simple. Unless staff and children have some clear idea about their respective and specific roles, however, the role confusion which occurs can become very bewildering and sometimes damaging to the life of the group.

The most obvious roles in a residential community are those concerned with authority and leadership and any attempt to analyse the pattern of roles in the group will tend to start with the head. His role, even as leader, however, will be composite and varied. The children may perceive him as ultimate authority or ultimate benefactor, someone to control them or someone to indulge them. Staff may also perceive the head as controller or facilitator or may look to him for support, encouragement, and expertise. The head of a therapeutic group will no doubt attempt to meet all these expectations at some point but will usually adopt one specific style of leadership to govern the community. In deciding on a particular style to adopt the head will be influenced by two broad considerations: first, by the expectations of the people who appointed him leader and the expectations inherent in the task itself; second, by his own personality. Ideally the two sets of 'needs' will be compatible, though at any given moment the behaviour of the leader may be

*Figure 1(1)* The nomothetic or organizational dimension in role behaviour

organizational (nomothetic) dimension

personal (idiographic) dimension

Reprinted with permission of Macmillan Publishing Co. Inc. from *Administrative Theory in Education* by Andrew W. Halpin. Copyright © 1958 Andrew W. Halpin.

dominated by one consideration more than the other. Owens (1970:54) designed *Figure 1(1)* to illustrate what he called the nomethetic or organizational element in role behaviour and the idiographic or personal dimension leading to observed behaviour. In a residential community which is aiming to provide a therapeutic milieu and where the leader is also a resident and therefore dependent on the community for a much greater proportion of his complete life than someone who goes out to work from nine to five, his style of leadership will tend to reflect his personality and personal needs quite as much as the specific demands of the organization. Thus it is observable that therapeutic communities are as different organizationally as the people who lead them. If we accept White and Lippit's (1960:319) well-known categorization of the three main styles of leadership – authoritarian, democratic and *laissez-faire* and their experimental results on group member reaction under each of the styles – it is interesting to note that most leaders of therapeutic residential communities claim to operate on a democratic model. White and Lippit found that under author-itarian leadership, where all policy was determined by the leader and he remained aloof from active group participation, the group worked well while he was present but disintegrated in his absence. Under democratic leadership, where all policies were a matter for discussion by the group and members were involved in decision making, with the leader very much a group member, it was found that the group could work effectively with or without the leader's presence and members achieved more satisfaction in being a member of the group. The *laissez-faire* group, where there was complete freedom for group or individual decision-making but where the leader opted out of involvement, did not work well together and members did not achieve much satisfaction.

A particular style of leadership invariably leads to the development of an organizational structure which can be placed somewhere along the mechanistic–organic continuum described by Burns and Stalker (1961). An authoritarian style of leadership is usually associated with a mechanistic organization and a democratic style of leadership with an organic organization. Neither of these systems is 'good' or 'bad' in its own right. What is important, to use Richard Balbernie's expression, is the 'matching of agreement of organization to task' (Balbernie 1966:61). Where the task is highly predictable and stable, a mechanistic system, which is based on rigid task definition and role structure, is often the more effective. In a residential community, however, the task is rarely completely certain and the primary task of therapy continually demands from staff imaginative and creative responses. An organic system, which is not dependent on a rigid structure and hierarchical roles, but encourages creative and innovative thinking and problem solving, would seem to provide a better fit of organization to task and would demand a more democratic style of leadership.

In a residential community, where personal satisfaction is essential for each member if working on the primary task of therapy is to be efficient, the leader is likely to achieve this in direct proportion to the degree in which he (a) enables each member to play an important and valued role in the community, (b) has an efficient system of communication so that each member is fully aware of what is happening in the group, (c) builds into the organization regular support and encouragement, and (d) is also a lively, strong and enthusiastic member of the group himself.

How, in practical terms, are these objectives achieved in a residential community? Communities vary, of course, in their basic structure. Some are organized into several sub-groups based on, for example, age, sex, needs, and some are run as one group, but, whatever the structure, lines of communication need to be built into the system and not just left to chance. The same applies to staff support. It is not enough to step in as leader when there is a crisis. Praise and support for each member of staff need to be given on a regular basis. In my own community we attempt to do this through regular meetings — staff with leader, staff with line manager — staff with social worker — whole staff meetings and staff with children meetings. Some communities achieve communication through written reports, logbooks, daily whole community meetings. The feeling that one is important enough to be informed of what is going on also helps one to feel valued and important and consequently to be prepared to invest heavily in the smooth running of the organization.

In a residential community, perhaps more than in any other type of organization, the leader needs to be aware of and to facilitate two major forces at work within the group. Bales (1958:78), in his extensive research on the interaction in groups, describes these as the force related to the task and its solution, and the force relating to the sentient system, i.e. the group atmosphere and feeling. When thinking of my own role, as leader of a residential community, in relation to the sentient system, I often see myself as the juggler in a music hall act who has a number of plates spinning on top of poles and who has to keep them all spinning by rushing from plate to plate as they start to slow down!

Other important authority/support roles will be played by the deputy head and sub-group leaders. The role of the deputy is never an easy one as he, in a sense, has to serve two masters. He is seen by the head as support and substitute for himself in carrying out policy, while the rest of the staff and children see the deputy as someone who mediates between themselves and the head and also represents their interests. Again I would stress the added pressures on individual staff who both live and work in a residential community. The ability to form a satisfactory personal as well as professional relationship with colleagues with whom one also lives can add to role confusion. For example, a member of staff is at one moment acting in a subservient or supporting role to the head and in the next moment is chastising the head's children for digging up the lawn or is beating the head at golf! As with all the aspects of a therapeutic community discussed above, it is important, when functioning in the many and varied roles the situation demands, to be able to act with tolerance and honesty. In my experience it is much better, should there be a conflict of roles and personalities in the group, that they be brought to the surface and discussed and resolved openly than be repressed and left to fester and so undermine the security of the group. This, of course, relies on the maturity and insight of the staff and particularly, perhaps, of the head and deputy. Where there is a value system which rewards tolerance and understanding, however, conflicts should be short-lived, leaving staff with enough of the vital energy required to concentrate on the task of creating a therapeutic community.

The roles in which the children find themselves in the group will be discussed later in relation to specific group therapies but for the moment suffice it to say that once again the children's role system is likely to reflect something of the staff system in, for example, the power it gives to leaders, its ability to deal with deviants and its use of distinct roles, such as scapegoat, clown, shop steward.

PLANNING TREATMENT

Once a child has settled into a residential community and been helped to feel that his new home is one in which he may ask for and receive acceptance and help with his problems, the residential social worker is in a position to plan the specific forms of treatment he feels may be appropriate for the child. Having received the maximum amount of information about the child through case histories, interviews, and tests, the residential therapist is able to construct a hypothesis about the child he is going to treat. This hypothesis should be talked through with all staff who will come into close contact with the child and ideally with the child's family and, in a simplified fashion, with the child himself. It is important to remember that, like assessment, treatment planning is a continuous process and should be open to regular review. The original hypothesis is likely to be quite simple as the child is still very much an unknown quantity and may begin to behave and respond differently from expectations which have been built up about him simply because he is now in a new environment where, hopefully, some of the pressures and anxieties from his past have been removed. It is helpful to write down this first hypothesis and to record subsequent modifications as this enables the therapist to formulate treatment goals. Many therapists then present these goals to the child in the form of a contract which he may be asked to sign.

Some communities also ask the parents to enter into a contract to work together with the child and staff and this may also be written down and signed. The following is an illustration of what I mean by a hypothesis and its implications for treatment:

*Collated information about Ian*:

*Age* − 14 − small for his age.

*Development stage* − Adolescence.

*Implications of developmental stage* − anti-authority feelings, approach-avoidance conflict towards independence − sometimes he wishes to be treated as a child but at other times wishes to be considered grown up. He is struggling to develop a sense of identity and an interest in sexual relationships is growing rapidly.

*Family*:

*Mother* − Deserted Ian and father when Ian was five years old.

*Father* − Caring but weak and inconsistent in handling Ian. Re-married a woman with a strong domineering personality, one son.

*Stepmother* − Favours her own son and rejects Ian. Frequently asks father to choose between her and Ian, threatening to leave home if Ian returns.

*Siblings*:

*Brother* − much older, in the army.

*Stepbrother* — seen as the 'goody' in relation to Ian as the 'baddy'.

*Presenting problems*:

Delinquency, disruptive in school; aggressive at home, cannot make friends, bullies younger children.

*Potential strengths*:

Deep affection for father and brother — good at sport — can be helpful.

*Educational standard*:

*Intelligence* — low average.
*Basic skills* — reading — average, numberwork — below average, art work — poor, craft and woodwork — good.

*Hypothesis*:

Ian, having suffered two severe rejections by mother and stepmother, will have a low self-image and will find it very difficult to trust women. Having experienced insecurity from having a weak father, he will look to men to be strong.

*Implications for treatment*:

Early goals will be to increase Ian's self-esteem, to enable him to work through his ambivalence towards women and to provide a satisfactory male figure in his life on whom he can model.

Some of the early treatment goals specified for a particular child may only be achievable in the context of a one-to-one relationship with a member of staff. Children who have never experienced the security and warmth of unconditional acceptance from any adult may need to build up and test out this primary relationship with a chosen member of staff before they are ready for group therapy. These children, described by therapist Barbara Docker-Drysdale (1973:33) as 'frozen' or 'unintegrated' children, do not have the ego strength to enable them to participate 'safely' in group therapy and the residential community will need to design suitable structures for individual treatment of such children before introducing them to any form of group therapy. Once a group of children has reached a point where the individuals have developed some capacity to trust staff, peers, and themselves, the residential therapist is in a position to decide which form of group therapy to use.

I believe that it is desirable, and perfectly possible, to provide more than one type of group therapy within the same establishment and that the secret of success lies in selecting the most suitable therapy for the assessed needs and problems of each child. As the child matures and starts to cope successfully with his most pressing problems, it may be advisable to introduce him into a different therapy group.

Three group therapies (Transactional Analysis, Behaviour Modification Group Therapy, and Encounter Group Therapy) will now be examined in some detail, first as personality theories with implications and significance for staff and second as a practical method of group therapy for children, with suggestions for running group therapy sessions.

SUMMARY

In this chapter there has been a very brief attempt to examine some of the important characteristics of a therapeutic residential community as a setting within which a variety of individual and group therapies can take place. I have stressed the importance of the relationships of the staff with each other, as well as with the children, as a satisfactory model for the whole community, and I have discussed the need to have a clear definition of tasks and an understanding of roles. Ways in which the physical environment can be used to encourage therapy were explored and the importance of clear and viable task definition was emphasized. Residential social workers were seen to have special needs compared with field workers in that their personal lives will inevitably impinge on their professional lives because they live and work in the same setting. The main theme of the chapter has been that children will learn what they live — if they live with despair they will become desperate; if they live with hope and trust they will become hopeful and trusting.

# 2 Group Therapy: Transactional Analysis

'Transactional Analysis', strictly speaking, is an expression which refers to the technique of analysing the transactions or exchanges which take place between two people. It is also used to describe, collectively, the various major aspects of personality theory developed by Eric Berne (1910–70). Berne's theory of personality was born out of his early training as a psychoanalyst and his philosophy which had, at its core, the firm belief that there are no 'born losers', that everyone can become a 'winner' and that each person is essentially 'O.K.'.

It is this belief in the positive aspects of personality development and the ability of man to make decisions about, and to have the ability to change, his destiny which makes Transactional Analysis (commonly abbreviated to T.A.) attractive to therapists working either with individuals or with groups.

One of Berne's early moments of inspiration happened when he realized that the patients he was treating through psychoanalysis could be observed to be in a different type of ego state in different situations or in different relationships and that these ego states could be described as 'Parent', 'Adult' or 'Child'. He gives the example of a successful lawyer whom he was treating. (1961:33)

'(He) raised his family decently, did useful community work, and was popular socially. But in treatment he often did have the attitude of a little boy. Sometimes during the hour he would ask: "Are you talking to the lawyer or to the little boy?" When he was away from his office or the court room, the little boy was very apt to take over. He would retire to a cabin in the mountains away from his family, where he kept a supply of whiskey, morphine, lewd pictures, and guns. There he would indulge in childlike fantasies, fantasies he had had as a little boy, and the kinds of sexual activity which are commonly labeled "infantile".'

When the lawyer was doing community work he was copying his father who had also worked for the community; when he was in court he was very rational and adult in his behaviour; when he was relaxing away from his family he was very child-like. After many similar observations of patients, Berne formulated his theory of ego states and the first principle of his theory of personality is the analysis and understanding of how a person develops his three possible ego states and how he uses these to communicate, or mis-communicate, with others.

THE CHILD EGO

The Child Ego is the part of our personality with which we are all born and contains, like the Freudian Id, the reflex and spontaneous needs and drives, both physical and emotional. Three different facets of the Child Ego are formed from birth onwards and remain as part of our personality throughout life. The first part is our 'Free' or 'Natural' Child and is the part of us which responds spontaneously to any given stimulus and does not take into account the reactions of parent or authority figures. In its positive form the Free Child is responsible for the 'fun' and spontaneous creativity we enjoy in life. In its more negative form it is responsible for outbursts of temper and uncontrolled destructive impulses.

The second part of our Child Ego is the Adapted Child and is the part of the child which adapts to the demands and expectations of parent figures. This part of the ego responds in childhood and throughout life as if parent figures were keeping a critical eye upon it. It is much more inhibited than the Free Child but, like the Free Child, can act in a way which is either positive or negative in its effect on the personality. In its positive form it helps the child to develop acceptable manners and to be considerate towards others. In its negative form it may influence the personality to become over-compliant or to take on board beliefs about the self which are not true. For example, a child who adapts to his parents' repeated statement that he is not very intelligent may find himself conforming, in spite of his actual high intelligence, to this view of himself and behaving accordingly. Woollams and Brown (1979:15) describe the three typical Adapted Child behaviours as 'Helpful, Hurtful and Helpless' and suggest that, by being 'compliant, industrious or rebellious', the Adapted Child is acting in a way which will 'pay off' with parent figures.

The third aspect of the Child Ego has been called the Little Professor and is the part of the Child Ego which develops an intuitive and creative approach to life in the interests of the child's manipulation of his environment to best meet his needs. Woollams and Brown (1979:12) have described the Little Professor as the first Adult or thinking part which 'allows the pre-verbal infant to "know" how mother feels and gives him a method of figuring out what to do to get along'. This part of our Child Ego, though essentially developed during childhood, stays with us throughout life as our ability to be both curious and creative and as the ability to trust our intuition.

When observing many of the children who find themselves in a residential community, having been assessed as in need of therapy, the aspects of the Child Ego most apparent in their personality and behaviour are those which bring the least rewards. The Free Child has no ability to have harmless fun but seeks expression through destructive games. How often do we say of a child in our care, 'He doesn't know when to stop — when I have a game which starts out as fun with him he always takes it too far'? Similarly, the Adapted Child part of such a child's Ego will be acted out through rebellious anti-authority behaviour and very few of these children have a sound Little Professor to guide them successfully through life's pitfalls. It is important, therefore, when using a T.A. model of therapy to help a child, that we provide opportunities for the positive aspects of the Child Ego to be developed as these will help to determine, in turn, the development of his Parent Ego and Adult Ego.

THE PARENT EGO

The Parent Ego is the part of the personality which has taken into itself the attitudes, commands, and prohibitions which the child experienced in his early relationships with parents and strong parental/authority figures. Like the Child Ego it can function in ways which are positive and helpful to the personality generally or in ways which are negative and less helpful. When parental behaviour is observed, it can be seen to fall into two broad categories: 'nurturing' and 'critical'. The Nurturing Parent functions positively when providing warmth, acceptance, care, and reassurance and negatively when overprotecting or being over-permissive with the child. The Critical Parent is also the Controlling Parent and functions positively when providing strong protection, useful principles by which to make judgements, and a powerful model of a 'good parent'. The Critical Parent functions negatively when it attacks the self-esteem of the child and is over-demanding and over-punitive. The developing child will incorporate into the Parent part of his ego the most significant aspects of his parental figures and will carry these and add to them throughout his life. He will find it difficult to eradicate these 'tapes' no matter how irrational he may later decide them to be. I, for example, still feel, in the Parent part of my ego, that it is wrong to go to the cinema on a Sunday because my Methodist parents held this view very strongly. My rational adult finds this view totally irrational but my Parent tape remains the stronger.

The implications, for many of our children in residential care, of the power of their Parent tapes are highly significant for therapy planning. The majority of our children will have been exposed, either to inadequate nurturing from parents or, as in the case of many school-phobic children, to over-protective and stultifying nurturance. Similarly, the Critical Parent they have experienced is likely to have been either very punitive and harsh or not controlling enough. If we are to help children, through T.A., to modify or expand their Parent Ego to include the positive aspects, it will be necessary to provide enough 'good' parental experiences for the child to be able to store an adequate supply of these 'good' tapes to counterbalance his damaging previous experiences. Fortunately, the Child Ego can continue to assimilate new information into the Parent Ego throughout life and, in a residential community, staff are in a very strong position to provide this once they have established themselves, for a particular child, as credible parent figures. Equally, staff who do not use this power responsibly can reinforce a child's previous bad experiences and strengthen the force of the child's negative parenting potential in a way which will be acted out destructively in relation to his own children when the child has grown up and become a parent.

THE ADULT EGO

The third part of the personality identified by Berne is the Adult Ego. This is the part of the personality which starts life as the Little Professor and gradually develops into the rational, thinking part of the personality. The more factual information that is stored up in the Adult the more efficient the Adult will become in helping the person to make sound and objective decisions about life. Of course the Adult will not only gather information from outside the person but will also be aware of the messages being sent out by the Child Ego and Parent Ego. It will be able to analyse these messages and filter out those which could be inhibiting or detrimental to the problem-solving function of the Adult. The Adult is like a computer in the way it processes data fed into it and it is the personality's mechanism for calculating probabilities. The continued development of the Adult is vital to the mental health and ability to cope successfully with life, 'as it is', for the individual. Children in a residential community often have more than the average share of problems to solve in life and it is therefore even more important for them, than for more fortunate children, to develop, early, an Adult Ego which can make the most constructive decisions. Unfortunately, due to the overpowering influence of predominantly destructive Child and Parent Egos, they often find it more difficult to develop their Adult and to survive happily in their environment. It is important therefore for staff to build, into treatment, opportunities for children to be helped to learn, to think, and to conceptualize. From this point of view, education, in its widest sense, is not a luxury for the emotionally disturbed child but an essential, and should be seen and planned for as a vital element in a treatment programme. Staff should allot time to talking with children and to helping them to expand their capacity for logical and abstract thought as well as for the process called 'intuition'. Many children in care have been language deprived amongst their many other deprivations and this will hamper the growth of their Adult Ego.

James and Jongeward (1975:48) describe the Adult Ego as the 'executive of the personality' in that it can make decisions about what it is appropriate to use from the Parent or Child Ego. They maintain that the Adult Ego is using its executive power when it acts as:

'Referee when there is inner conflict between the Parent and Child;
. . . protector of the Child when it feels threatened;
sets reasonable goals and determines procedures for achieving the goals;
selects and uses Parent behaviours appropriately;
selects and uses Child behaviours appropriately;
learns new ways of thinking and acting.'

Without the continuing development of a healthy Adult Ego, the growing child will be unable to select appropriate responses to the myriad stimuli in his life and will be increasingly in need of therapy.

TRANSACTIONAL ANALYSIS

Having identified the three Ego States which combine to form the personality, Berne and his followers went on to examine the way we use the Parent, Adult, and Child to communicate or make transactions with other people. In any given exchange, verbal or non-verbal, between two people, each of them will be cathecting, i.e. using, one of the three ego states. It is possible to observe three types of transaction: complementary, crossed,

*Figure 2(1a)* Complementary transaction

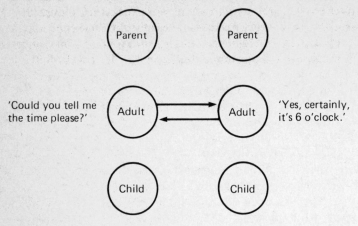

*Figure 2(1b)* Parallel complementary transaction (child ego)

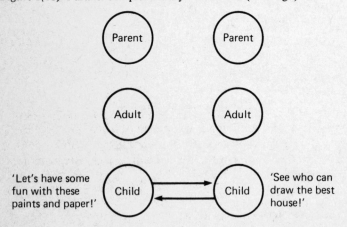

and ulterior, and each of these transactions can be more or less satisfactory according to its appropriateness to the messages being conveyed.

## Complementary transactions

Complementary transactions take place when the message

conveyed by one person is accurately understood and responded to by another person. Very often these transactions are parallel in that they are conveyed between the same ego states, see *Figure 2(1a)*. Parallel Complementary transactions can occur between each ego state, see *Figures 2(1b)* and *2(1c)*.

*Figure 2(1c)* Parallel complementary transaction (parent ego)

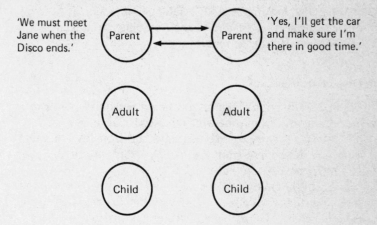

'We must meet Jane when the Disco ends.'

'Yes, I'll get the car and make sure I'm there in good time.'

*Figure 2(2)* Complementary transactions between different ego states

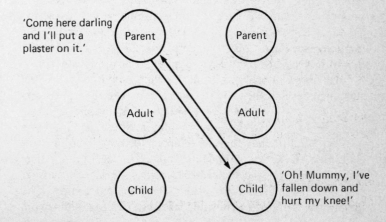

'Come here darling and I'll put a plaster on it.'

'Oh! Mummy, I've fallen down and hurt my knee!'

Complementary transactions need not take place between the same ego states; the criterion for the transaction being complementary is that the messages sent are appropriate and correctly understood by both people, see *Figure 2(2)*. In all close, satisfactory relationships there will be a preponderance of complementary transactions and in unsatisfactory relationships insufficient.

Most of the children in residential communities are described as being unable to make 'good relationships' and in T.A. terms this can be seen to be due to their inability to make enough complementary transactions.

## Crossed transactions

Crossed transactions take place when a person responds to a message from an ego state which the sender of the message did not expect, e.g. one person sends a message from his Adult Ego expecting a response from the other person's Adult Ego, see *Figure 2(3a)*, *(3b)*, *(3c)*, and *(3d)*.

Many of the children in our care seem to be 'stuck' in one ego state, e.g. the rebellious 'adapted child' or the over-dependent 'adapted child'. These children will find it difficult to interpret any messages sent to them by staff as anything but critical and rejecting. It is then very hard for staff who think they have been sending out 'nurturing parent' messages not to retaliate, because of their own hurt at being misunderstood, by acting either as a punitive parent or even as an angry child! For example, (see *Figure 2(3b)*) a member of staff sees a child about to hurt himself by falling off a pyramid of boxes on which he is balanced precariously and, from this Nurturing Parent Ego, the staff member tells the child to come down. The child, who perceives him as a Critical Parent, shouts back angrily, from his Free Child Ego, 'You're always trying to spoil my fun!'. The member of staff may then be tempted to reply from his own Child Ego, 'O.K. fall off and hurt yourself – see if I care!'. The child has not received the correct 'caring' message in the first place because of his expectations about parent figures. The member of staff, instead of using his Adult Ego to explain to the

*Figure 2(3a)* Crossed transactions

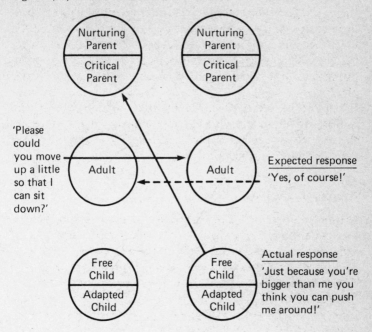

child's Adult Ego the reasons for his first remark resorts to using his own Child Ego. The transaction is crossed and the child's propensity for expecting the worst from adults has been reinforced.

Whereas many crossed transactions are unhelpful to a relationship, sometimes it is constructive to cross a transaction in order to improve the communication. For instance, (see *Figure 2(3c)*) had the member of staff in the previous example been able to communicate from his Adult Ego to the child's Adult Ego, the transaction and the relationship would have made progress.

It is often possible for staff by using an ego state not expected by the child to manipulate a crossed transaction so that the child who felt 'not O.K.' in the initial transaction can be helped to feel more 'O.K.'; see *Figure 2(3d)*.

*Figure 2(3b)* Crossed transaction − negative

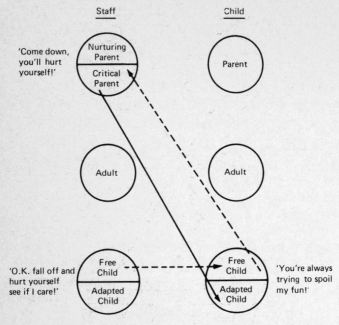

*Figure 2(3c)* Crossed transaction − positive

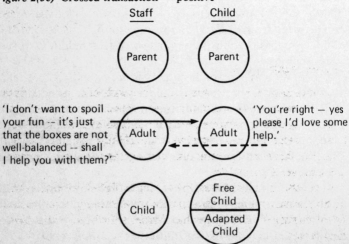

*Figure 2(3d)* Manipulated crossed transaction − positive

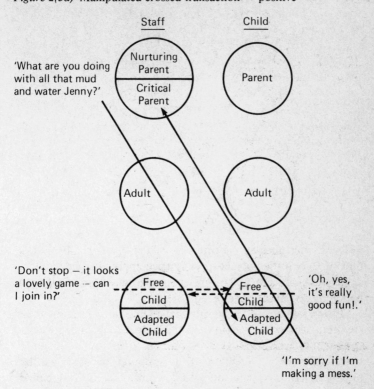

## Ulterior transactions

Ulterior transactions are transactions which take place at two levels − an overt or social level and a covert or psychological level. They differ from crossed transactions in that more than two ego states are used at the same time. Many transactions, for example, have an overt social message and a covert sexual message, see *Figure 2(4)*.

In an ulterior transaction the outcome of the transaction will be determined more by the psychological message than by the social message and may or may not be satisfactory as a communication.

*Figure 2(4)* Ulterior transaction

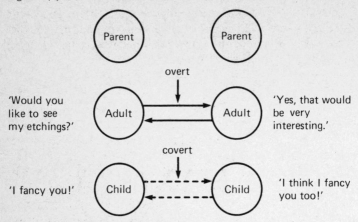

The hidden message is often conveyed non-verbally by the tone of voice or the facial expression accompanying the remark. A person's posture or gestures may also alter drastically the apparent verbal message being sent.

I have often noticed in a residential community how adept the children become at picking up the hidden messages in their transactions with staff. It is very difficult for staff to disguise successfully either feelings of disapproval or approval by relying solely on verbal communications. A little boy called Paul springs to my mind. Paul's language and behaviour were anti-social in the extreme and he seemed to be perpetually on the receiving end of Critical Parent messages. Paul, however, had a charm and lovable quality which were irresistible and consequently the Critical Parent remarks made to him were invariably accompanied by a subtle warmth and approval which completely belied the words used!

Similarly, staff can send messages which are verbally approving but, because of a covert disapproval felt by the sender, do not fool the child for a moment. As many of our children have a very poor self-image they often wear a permanent label conveying a 'loser' message about themselves rather like a message on a tee-shirt. Whatever their overt transactions with others this is the message which comes through, e.g. 'I'm tough', 'I'm unlovable', 'I'm dumb'. The ulterior transactions made by these children are not satisfactory or satisfying but may be the only ones of which they are capable until they have been helped to feel O.K.

## Strokes

One of the most important concepts within T.A. is that everyone is born to be a 'winner' and has the capacity to feel that he himself and the other people with whom he interacts are O.K. To be O.K. in T.A. terms is to value yourself and to feel that you are a worthwhile person in your own right and can take a realistic view of your own strengths and weaknesses. Similarly, to feel that others are O.K. is to accord them respect and acceptance and to be able to perceive their strengths and weaknesses realistically.

New-born babies are in a symbiotic relationship with the mother in which they, for a short time, are not two separate people but form one person between them (Winnicot 1965:40). As the infant matures he begins to separate himself out from this very close relationship and to develop a personality in his own right. If the emotional environment is adequately supportive he will gain an increasing self-confidence in his own worth and ability and will not fear growing independence. In T.A. terms, he will feel O.K. and will be in a position to accept that other people are O.K. If the early mother–baby relationship was not satisfactorily symbiotic the baby will feel cheated and may spend much of his childhood or even his life seeking this type of relationship and proving himself incapable of true independence based on a feeling of self-worth and self-confidence.

The ideal 'life position' from which to think, feel, and act in relation to others is 'I'm O.K. – You're O.K.'. The degree to which we are able to feel this is determined by the amount and type of feedback and approval or disapproval for ourselves which we experience from birth onwards. In T.A. language, this feedback is called 'stroking' and is analagous, in psychological terms, with a baby's need for physical contact or 'stroking' in order to survive.

In the days when institutional care for orphan babies involved very little physical contact many babies died from a condition called marasmus, a shrivelling of the spine, which was a direct result of the lack of physical touch. Transactional analysts maintain that an individual whose need for psychological stroking is not met will shrivel up and 'die' emotionally. The personality who is seriously deprived in this way will develop no capacity to feel O.K. and possibly no capacity to feel that others are O.K. On the other hand he may feel, from his own feeling of low self-worth, that others are O.K. but he is not O.K. If he projects the 'bad' and inadequate feelings onto others, he may feel that he is O.K. but others are not O.K. The four possible stances to take at any given moment are in *Figure 2(5)*.

*Figure 2(5)* Possible psychological life positions

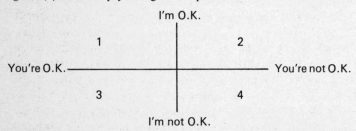

The first position, 'I'm O.K. − You're O.K.', is the healthy position from which to view oneself and others realistically and positively. It does not mean that the person in this position will not perceive problems or negative aspects of his relationships and transactions but that when he does so he will seek to deal with them by using his Adult Ego or the constructive parts of his Child Ego or Parent Ego.

The second position, 'I'm O.K. − You're not O.K.', is the paranoid position from which a person feels himself to be persecuted or victimized by others. This feeling then gives him justification for blaming and punishing others and is at the root of many delinquent or criminal behaviours.

The third position, 'I'm not O.K. − You're O.K.', is the

depressive position from which a person feels himself to be weak and helpless in relation to others and may cause him to become over-dependent or, if the feeling of failure and inadequacy is extreme, suicidal.

The fourth position, 'I'm not O.K. – You're not O.K.', is the hopeless position which could lead the individual, at its extreme, to either suicide or homicide from a feeling that there is nothing to live for or nothing to lose.

Each person in life has a 'favourite' psychological position which is the one he adopted very eary in life and is based on his early experiences of being psychologically stroked. He may take up each of the positions from time to time but will spend most of his life in his favoured position – especially when under any type of threat to his ego.

Strokes can be given unconditionally for 'being' or conditionally for 'doing' and can be positive, negative, or artificial. As strokes are essential for the growth of the personality, a baby or child who does not receive sufficient positive strokes will seek negative or artificial strokes as preferable to no strokes at all.

Many of the children who are in residential care have had an early history of emotional deprivation and have consequently learnt to survive by seeking negative strokes in place of the positive strokes they have been denied. They will settle themselves into life positions in which they or others are decidedly not O.K. and consequently will continue to receive a preponderance of negative strokes. It is important for staff, therefore, to be able to provide a sufficient supply of positive strokes to enable these children to alter their view of life to one which is more positive about self as well as about others. As much of the behaviour of the children will make conditional stroking difficult for staff, early therapy will include a high percentage of unconditional positive stroking for the child as a worthwhile person in his own right.

It can be observed that people in authority roles in relation to children, e.g. houseparents and teachers, find it easier to comment on the negative aspects of a child's personality and behaviour than on the positive aspects. If a child is 'being' and 'doing' what is acceptable this very often goes without comment.

It is vital for staff therefore to widen their capacity to give, quite consciously, positive strokes and to comment on acceptable as well as on unacceptable behaviour.

T.A. stresses the importance of the therapist being aware of his own stroke economy in order to be able to give the necessary strokes his job demands. The more positive strokes a therapist has received and continues to receive the more likely he is to be able to give them freely to others. It is therefore important for him to learn to ask for positive strokes for himself and to be able to accept them when they are given. It is perhaps a peculiarly English habit to be unable to accept compliments, i.e. positive strokes, gracefully. Often when complimented on one's appearance or attributes the temptation is to deprecate the remark. If we are to become vigorous and healthy residential therapists we should not be ashamed to seek and accept the positive strokes which will give us the feeling of self-respect from which to respect others and to give positive strokes.

A useful exercise for staff to do in relation to their own pattern of giving, receiving, asking for, and refusing to give positive and negative strokes is the Stroking Profile devised by McKenna (1975), reproduced in *Figure 2(6)*.

Steiner (1974) christened the three possible types of strokes, i.e. positive, negative, and artificial strokes, 'Warm Fuzzies', 'Cold Pricklies' and 'Plastic Fuzzies' respectively and the way staff can use these concepts in relation to therapy with children will be explored more fully in Chapter 3. Suffice it for now to say that Warm Fuzzies (positive strokes) are messages which help the child to feel 'O.K.'. Cold Pricklies (negative strokes) are messages which make the child feel 'not O.K.'. Plastic Fuzzies (artificial strokes) are messages which seem to be saying 'You're O.K.' but due to the tone of voice or some non-verbal accompaniment are really saying, 'You're not O.K.', e.g. a teacher saying to a child in a sarcastic voice, 'Well, you're a real genius!'

For the development of a healthy personality each of the three ego states, Parent, Adult, Child, will need to receive a plentiful supply of positive strokes. The strokes needed for the Parent Ego will be similar to the types of strokes needed by

*Figure 2(6)* Stroking profile

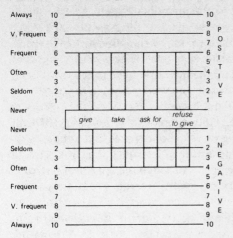

Instructions:

1. Rate yourself in each of these categories (*give, take, ask for, refuse to give*) as to how frequently you give, accept, ask for, and refuse to give positive recognition to and from others.
2. Do the same on the negative scale. (The negative and positive scales tend to have an inverse relationship.)
3. In rating yourself, consider *all* the strokes you give, take, etc. For example, include soft strokes like 'Hi! How are you?' as well as heavy strokes like embraces and 'I love you.'
4. In the *refuse to give* category, ask yourself how often you say 'No' to what people ask or expect of you. On the negative scale, if you never refuse to point out someone's faults or errors, you would rate yourself as '0' – never refuse to give a negative stroke.
5. Think of all transactions as strokes. 'I want you to go to the dance with me Saturday' is *Asking For* recognition, and answering 'No, I'd rather go to a show' is *Refusing To Give*.

one's parents, e.g. for being thoughtful, good with money, constructively critical of self or others. The Child Ego will need those strokes which reinforce the positive aspects of, for the Free Child, imagination and creativity; for the Adapted Child, independence and politeness; for the Little Professor, being 'clever'. For the Adult Ego the strokes needed will be for the ability to think rationally and to collate and process information correctly.

Children who do not receive a plentiful supply of positive

strokes will learn to rely on negative strokes for survival, the result being that they will then find it extremely difficult to accept positive strokes when they are offered as they have never practised the ability to do so. It may well not be sufficient therefore for the residential therapist to offer a steady flow of positive strokes to a child; he may first have to teach the child through a long, slow, patient process to be able to accept that there are good things about himself.

Deprived or disturbed children may also find it very difficult to internalize and 'hang on to' good strokes and good experiences in order to build up a store of internal good strokes to fall back on when times are hard. Although the most useful strokes are those which come to us from the external world, the healthy personality will have a fund of remembered positive strokes on which he can draw when in need. Staff in a residential community will need this resource a great deal as, by the very nature of their work, they are unlikely to receive many positive strokes from the children, especially early in therapy. I would maintain, therefore, that it is essential for staff amongst themselves, and especially from those in authority, to give and receive positive strokes which help them to feel O.K. In one exercise that I have used with staff in particular we each have a piece of paper pinned to our backs and go round each member of the group writing a positive comment on the paper. These lists of positive remarks are then read out by each recipient and can be stored away to be consulted at moments when the current supply of positive strokes seems low!

A concept which is closely allied in T.A. to the concept of Stroking is that of psychological trading stamps. Woollams and Brown (1979:132) describe these stamps as 'saved-up feelings or strokes which people use to justify some later behaviour'. They are called trading stamps because they are collected and later cashed in for some prize like the stamps that used to be offered by many shops and garages. When negative strokes, or brown stamps, are collected they will be cashed in to justify a piece of negative behaviour on the part of the collector. For example, a child who has been bullied frequently will store up these negative experiences and use them later to justify his bullying of another child. When positive strokes, or gold stamps, are collected they will be cashed in to justify a piece of self-indulgence on the part of the collector. For example, a child who is a persistent truant may collect enough gold stamps by attending school for a week to justify to himself taking the next week off!

Both types of stamp collecting are unhelpful to the growth of the personality and it will be part of our task, as residential therapists, to help children to express positive and negative feelings directly, instead of saving them up for a later pay-off which, because it is inappropriate, does not help them to feel O.K. Many of our children are described as having 'a chip on the shoulder'. In T.A. terms this would be the equivalent of a brown-stamp collection and can be clearly seen to be harmful to a child's happy maturation.

## Games

Another way of gaining substitute strokes is through what Berne (1964) called 'psychological games'. He defines a game as 'an ongoing series of complementary ulterior transactions progressing to a well-defined outcome'. Most of the games identified by Berne started life as responses from the Parent Ego or Adapted Child Ego in a situation in which the child was not given permission to respond from his Free Child Ego. For example, a child who is continually put down as helpless by an over-critical and harsh parent may find that if he responds to this by using his Adapted Child Ego and wears a tee-shirt with 'I'm helpless and stupid, pity me' he will receive strokes which are apparently positive from people who wish to rescue him. However, because the child is transacting from a position of not O.K., the final pay-off in this type of transaction can never be totally satisfactory and will more likely be used to justify to the child his own feeling of low self-worth.

Woollams and Brown (1979:118) maintain that games are played for the following reasons:

'To acquire strokes — positive strokes may be acquired in the early moves of the game, and negative strokes always accompany the pay-off. A "good" game is sometimes referred to as one in which the amount of pleasant strokes exchanged in the early phases of the game exceeds the amount of negative strokes which accompany the pay-off. However, these games are not really "good", since they maintain a not-OK life position.

To maintain one's frame of reference.

To collect stamps.

To confirm parental injunctions and further the life script.

To maintain the person's life position by "proving" that self and others are not-OK.

To provide a high level of stroke exchange while blocking intimacy and maintaining distance.

To "make" people predictable.'

Three of the most common roles which players of psychological games choose to adopt are those of Victim, Persecutor, and Rescuer. These roles are chosen, not as an appropriate response to a present stimulus, but as a response learnt in early childhood when the Free Child Ego was unable to express itself directly.

## Victim roles

People who choose to play the Victim role in a game have usually been subjected to numerous 'put down' transactions and received a preponderance of negative strokes from very early in their lives. This leads them, in order to retain a vestige of self-worth, to project the blame for what happens to them onto other people. Many of the children in a residential community find it difficult to take responsibility for their own behaviour and will always blame others when they find themselves in a criticized position. They have probably adopted this Victim role in response to very real harsh critical parenting and it is very difficult for staff to help such children to see that criticism of a piece of behaviour does not necessarily mean criticism of the child as a person who is essentially O.K. Helping a disturbed child to make the imaginative leap to a position in which he can take responsibility and, if necessary, punishment for his own misdemeanours without losing his essential feeling that he is O.K. as a person can only be attempted by staff when they have supported a child through an initial period of projection. For example, a child coming into a residential community, who has a long history of showing aggression to staff and other children, is likely to be chastized for violent behaviour which is producing an intolerable threat to other children. He will perhaps retaliate by becoming even more aggressive or by trying to lay the blame on another child. The member of staff dealing with the child then has the option of responding from his Critical Parent Ego to the child's Adapted Child Ego by chastizing him further or, if he is in tune with the child's desperate need to feel O.K., he can low-key the incident, perhaps by making a joke, which will allow the child to climb down from his aggressive perch and apologize without loss of face. For instance, I observed just such an incident in my residential community recently when a boy was objecting aggressively to being punished for something for which he was undoubtedly to blame. The member of staff dealing with him, instead of losing his temper and patience, suddenly started to chuckle and said, 'Never mind, Mark. I know you feel badly done to over this but just think of all the lovely times you've done something wrong and haven't been caught or punished!' Mark, inwardly reminiscing no doubt, also began to smile and the incident was over with, neither the member of staff nor the child losing his feeling of being O.K. This type of child will be helped to relinquish his Victim role when he has received sufficient positive strokes from staff and peers to enable him to experience fair criticism without losing all his sense of self-worth.

**Victim games**

*Kick Me*

Kick Me is a game in which one of the players continually sets himself up to be put down. He may, for instance, always be late or blatantly disobey rules, or act, quite deliberately, in a stupid way. How often do staff say of children like this, 'He just asks for trouble'? It is very hard for staff not to enter into this game by playing 'persecutor' to the child's 'victim' and only a conscious effort to stay in an Adult Ego state and to try to make transactions with the child's Adult Ego state will prevent the game from being repeated *ad infinitum*.

## Wooden Leg

Wooden Leg is a game in which the Victim uses a real or imaginary handicap as an excuse for not doing or not trying to do something which is actually achievable. I have observed children with a real handicap of mild epilepsy or asthma deliberately induce attacks to avoid a difficult emotional, intellectual, or physical challenge. Again, staff may have to collude with this behaviour initially until they have helped the child to build up enough courage to face difficult situations without feeling that he is bound to fail, and to gain the confidence to ask for positive strokes for his Free Child Ego because he deserves them for being a worthwhile person in his own right and not because of his handicap. A child who enjoys playing Wooden Leg will be wearing a 'Poor Me' tee-shirt and, if delinquent, may resort to the 'I'm depraved on account I'm deprived' rationalization of his negative behaviour. He may also develop a belief in fate or evil jinxes and, instead of examining the reasons for his apparent accident proneness, will resort to a Victim complaint of 'Why does this always happen to me?'

## 'Yes, but,' game

A game which is not quite so obviously a Victim game but is also founded on a child's experience of over-critical and authoritarian parenting is the 'Yes, but,' game. In this game the Victim asks for advice or help from a parent figure but then raises objections to the advice and reinforces his feeling that there is no solution to the problem. Children in a residential community will often ask for advice about how to make friends or how to get on with their parents then when the member of staff seeks to give advice will reject it with a 'Yes, but,' response. If the member of staff replies in a 'What's the use of trying to help you?' vein he is colluding with the game and the child will feel justified in his expectations of victimization.

## Persecutor roles

In order to play a Victim game the player has to find someone who is prepared to play the role of Persecutor. People who find it easy to adopt this role have a highly developed Critical Parent Ego and seem to enjoy making other people feel inferior.

Staff in a residential community are in a very good position to play Persecutor games as they already have comparative strength and authority in relation to the children. It is a sad observation that certain staff can be seen to abuse this power and authority by continually 'putting down' the Free Child Ego of the children with whom they are working and enjoying the strokes for their own Critical Parent Ego which they gain from this process.

Very often a person who plays the role of Persecutor in games takes up this role to avoid the role of Victim. For example, a member of staff who feels that he will receive negative strokes from people in authority over him if he allows his Free Child Ego to express itself creatively will punish a child over-harshly for a piece of behaviour which he does, or would like to do, himself. Often the staff most critical and punitive over behaviours such as smoking and swearing exhibit these anti-social behaviours themselves.

In making others feel not O.K. Persecutors are seeking to make themselves feel more adequate at the expense of Victims who feel weaker and are seeking to play a Victim game. By standing next to someone who is very fat one is able to feel thin!

## Persecutor games

### Blemish

In the game of Blemish, the Persecutor player can be observed to be looking continually for minor faults in potential Victim players. Having seen real or imaginary faults the Persecutor criticizes not only the fault but the whole person, who then is made to feel not O.K.! In this game the Persecutor gives negative strokes only, Cold Pricklies, or pseudo-positive strokes, Plastic Fuzzies, such as, 'You look nice in that dress, but it does make you look a bit fat!'.

Children playing Blemish will delight in telling tales about their peers in an attempt to gain positive strokes for their own Adapted Child Ego. In reality, however, the game of Persecutor and Victim will not help either of the participants to feel O.K. as it is founded solely on an exchange of negative or artificial good strokes.

## Now I've got you

The Persecutor who plays this game not only delights in criticizing his Victim but also sets up situations in which the Victim is bound to make a criticizable mistake. A member of staff, for example, may give inadequate or positively misleading instructions which will result in a child receiving punishment for breaking a rule or not behaving appropriately because of his lack of accurate instruction.

Staff may play the role of Persecutor in a game with a Victim, who is a member of staff in authority over them, by using energy to 'catch him out' making mistakes. The Persecutor gains a hollow satisfaction from making his superior feel inferior and the Victim can use this to excuse his own inadequacy in the situation by projecting the blame onto someone who is obviously prejudiced against him.

## Uproar

The most extreme type of Persecutor game is when two or more of the players all wish to be Persecutors. This can take place in a 'family' situation with members of staff and children all wishing to avoid the role of Victim by inviting someone else into it, or in a peer group, i.e. within a group of children or within a group of staff. The mutual negative stroking which takes place when two or more Persecutors confront each other usually finishes in a state of uproar in which all players eventually withdraw physically or psychologically and nobody feels O.K.

**Rescuer roles**

Players whose favourite role is that of Victim will often invite into the game people who enjoy the role of Rescuer. Rescuers in T.A. games are people who ostensibly seek to help others but whose real motivation is to keep the other person dependent on them and, by reinforcing their Victim feelings of inferiority, to maintain a feeling of superiority in relation to them. The temptation to keep children in a residential community over-dependent is very real for staff who use their job as therapists to seek positive strokes for their own ego through playing Rescuer to the children in their care. This is particularly true of staff who have insufficient sources of positive strokes in their own lives and rely on seeking strokes for their own Free Child and Parent Egos from the children whom they are treating. There is usually a ready supply of potential Victims in a residential community as there is also a ready supply of children who genuinely need rescuing. The help offered to children by staff only becomes a T.A. game when either Victim or Rescuer, or both, cannot let go of their roles of Victim and Rescuer at the appropriate time and the child is not allowed to assert his own self-worth and become independent from his Rescuer.

The origins of the need to play Rescuer in many social workers and teachers, whether residential or not, may lie in a Parent Ego tape which states that the person concerned can only be O.K. if he is helping or caring for others in a way which assumes that others are inferior. A type of pseudo-nurturing takes place in these games but, because neither the Victim nor the Rescuer wishes the game to reach a natural, positive conclusion of mutual interdependence and eventual independence the strokes exchanged are not really positive and neither player feels O.K.

**Rescuer games**

*I'm only trying to help*

The main characteristic of this game is that the Victim may not need or ask for advice or even want it when it is offered. The

Rescuer uses his authority in some area to offer advice which sounds well-meaning but is in fact very poor advice and it keeps the Victim dependent and feeling not O.K. For instance, a child in a residential community who has experienced a very difficult relationship with one or both of his parents but nevertheless wishes to retain respect for them and work towards achieving a more satisfactory relationship with them may be advised, by a Rescuer member of staff, not to place any trust in his parents and not to show them any affection. This member of staff may use his Rescuer role and authority vested in him professionally to manipulate the child into remaining a Victim in relation to his parents and an over-dependent child in relation to himself. Once again, the pay-off of the game is unsatisfactory for both players as the child will experience strong unresolved ambivalent feelings towards his parents and the member of staff who keeps him weak, and the member of staff will never have the satisfaction of seeing the child progress naturally from dependence to interdependence to independence.

## Why don't you?

This game is often played with a person who is playing the 'Yes, but,' game and has no real intention of taking the advice offered by the Rescuer playing 'Why don't you?' The Victim made a decision very early in life that parental and authority figures could not give adequate help and advice and therefore that no one knows the answers. By maintaining a seemingly weak and helpless stance in relation to others the Victim makes sure that the Rescuer always has a ready victim to be rescued but neither player is prepared to relinquish his role and the game only succeeds in making each of them feel not O.K. because the Victim has not been able to accept any real help and the Rescuer's advice has been rejected.

## Recognizing games

Woollams and Brown (1979:126) describe five different methods of recognizing and analysing games, ranging from formal game analysis to looking at the triangular transactions amongst Victim, Persecutor, and Rescuer which often take place when a game is being played. They state that 'games can be recognized by their repetitive occurrence, always beginning with a discount and always ending in racket feelings' — racket feelings being any feeling which 'results from a discount, justifies someone's not O.K. position, and does not successfully resolve the Free Child need or want' (1979:119).

Each game has a predictable sequence of events and feelings and James and Jongeward (1975:134) have evolved a game plan to help a therapist recognize a game when it is being played.

'The game plan focuses on predictable patterns and pay-offs. To use the game plan ask the following questions and write down the answers:
  What keeps happening over and over that leaves someone feeling bad?
  How does it start?
  What happens next?
  How does it end?
  How does each person feel when it ends?'

When a residential therapist realizes that a child is caught up in a constant series of games in a search for strokes he can either interpret the game to the child and help him to see that he can get real positive strokes by other methods or, if the child is too young or inarticulate to benefit from this, the therapist will simply divert the child from the game by providing him with enough unconditional positive strokes so that he no longer has any need of the game.

## Life scripts

An extension of the concept of psychological games is the T.A. concept of psychological scripts. Berne (1974:418) defined a psychological script as 'an ongoing program, developed in early childhood under parental influence, which directs the individual's behaviour in the most important aspects of his life'. While parents and the extended family are undoubtedly the most powerful influences on the type of script a child will base his life upon, other influences, such as the culture and sub-culture in which a child is reared and the expectations placed on a child's sex, also play their part. In our increasingly multi-racial society the script expectations of being, for example, Jewish, Negro, or Pakistani are tending to become more exag-gerated as minority ethnic groups struggle to survive. Some cultures, e.g. the Jewish culture, hand down from generation to generation a Victim script; some cultures, where domination of other races has figured highly in the past and present, hand down a Persecutor script, and still others have cast themselves in a script of Rescuer.

Sub-cultures within a racial culture are also responsible for propagating script messages and prejudices, e.g. northerners are suspicious of southerners, the Welsh of the English, the middle classes of the working classes, and Roman Catholics of Protestants.

Many families have a rigid set of expectations about what it is to be a man or a woman. Sex role definition is perhaps more flexible these days but on the whole attitudes and script decisions about e.g. boys being good at science and girls at the arts, or boys being physically aggressive and girls being passive, are still prevalent in many families.

The combined effect of the various influences on the growing child result in him conducting his life on what is primarily a winner script, a loser script, or possibly one which is really neither and, therefore, somewhat banal and unexciting.

### Creating the script

To return to Berne's definition of a psychological script as 'an ongoing program, developed in early childhood under parental influence, which directs the individual's behaviour in the most important aspects of his life', what exact processes take place in the development of the script?

There are two types of major script-deciding messages which parents and close authority figures give to children: permissions and injunctions. Permissions, as their name implies, allow children to be, to think, and to feel in particular ways which encourage the growth of their belief in themselves as winners and help them to feel confident that their life script will be predominantly successful and will enable them to feel that they, and others, are O.K. A parent who is handing down a winner's script to a child will firstly express positive feelings about his own life experience and by encouragement, praise, and positive strokes for each healthy aspect of the child's developing ego will, in turn, give the child permission to be happy and successful and enable him to grow.

Injunctions from parents to children are the reverse of permissions in that they are designed to inhibit growth and will be creating a 'don't succeed', 'you're a loser' type of script. Like permissions they will be to do with feeling, e.g. 'Don't get too close emotionally to other people, they'll only let you down!'; thinking, e.g. 'Don't try to understand yourself or others, life has no rhyme nor reason!'; and being, e.g. 'Don't think we need you, my boy, Mum and Dad managed quite well before you came along!'. These negative messages will convince the child that his life script is a loser's script and that he is basically not O.K. and nor are other people.

People make life script decisions in response to a combination of positive and negative inputs and will feel themselves to be winners in direct proportion to the predominance of positive messages received. As many of the children in a residential community will have come from families who have felt themselves to be working on a loser script, it is not surprising that they too often feel that life is stacked against them and that they in turn are bound to be losers. Therapy for such children often consists in helping them to change their script and to see that it is not inevitable for them to follow their family's unhappy script and continue the vicious circle of unhappy parents creating unhappy children who then grow up to be unhappy parents.

## Typical scripts

Eric Berne, when describing the most common types of scripts identifiable (1974:39), likened them to children's fairy tales whose major themes are love, hate, gratitude, and revenge.

Many of the children in our care could be said to be acting on a 'Cinderella Script', which gives them the expectations from life that other children will always have an easier time and be more favoured than they are unless some magic, rescuing Prince Charming comes along. Adolescent girls living on this script will often enter into a sexual or even marital relationship with the first man who shows an interest in them in the belief that he is Prince Charming, only to be disillusioned when it is perhaps too late and they have brought another potential loser child into the world.

Other children, particularly school-phobic and overdependent children will be working on a 'Peter Pan Script', which prescribes that they must never grow up and yet others may be working on a 'Princess and the Frog Script' which reinforces their feeling that, although they may feel themselves to be a handsome prince inside, other people will always find them unattractive and unlovable unless some magic process, outside their own control, provides the transforming kiss − in T.A. words, 'I'm O.K., you're not O.K.'

Another way of categorizing scripts is suggested by Woollams and Brown (1979:166), who classify scripts under Male and Female stereotypes as follows:

| Men | Women |
| --- | --- |
| Big Daddy | Mother Hubbard |
| Man in Front of the Woman | Plastic Woman |
| Playboy | The Woman behind the Man |
| Jock | Poor Little Me |
| Intellectual | Sleeping Beauty |
| Woman Hater | Nurse |

These stereotyping scripts are often handed down from father to son and mother to daughter and, whereas they may not always produce loser scripts, they are likely to produce banal scripts which leave the person feeling that surely life should have something a little more exciting to offer.

## Identifying and changing the script

When attempting to identify one's own script or that of a child in treatment, the simplest way is to start by asking questions about life history and life expectations with an emphasis on parental attitudes and expectations. Woollams and Brown (1979:162–63) suggest the following questions as suitable:

'What is your earliest memory?
What is the family story about your birth?
How were you named?
What was/is your nickname?
How old will you be when you die?
What will it say on your tombstone?
Describe yourself.
What was your mother's/father's main advice to you?
What did your mother/father want you to be?
What do you like most/least about yourself?
Did you ever feel that something might be wrong with you? If so, what?
Describe the bad feeling that you have had most often in your life.
What was your favorite childhood story/fairy tale/book/ hero/TV program?
What would "heaven on earth" be for you?
What do you wish your mother/father had done differently?
If by magic you could change anything about yourself just by wishing what would you wish for?
What do you want most out of life?
What famous person would you most want to be like?'

Children, and sometimes staff, in a residential community are often living life on either a loser script or a script which is unrealistic in that it is acted out in the constant hope that there will be a magical intervention at some point in life which will make one a winner, e.g., 'When I win the pools . . .!' or 'My boy friend will marry me and we'll live happily ever after!'

The magical intervention offered by T.A. therapy is not so much magic as hard work but it does offer the possibility of changing a loser script into a winner script to the child who, with much support from caring and constructive adults, is prepared to ask for and accept the positive strokes which will help him to feel 'I'm O.K. You're O.K.'

In a therapeutic community a new experience leading to a new script will be offered if the community is achieving its goals. If these goals are not clear or prove unattainable, the community will be merely providing a different setting in which staff and children will live out their old unsatisfactory scripts.

In order to formulate and achieve T.A. treatment goals for both therapist and child it is usual to draw up a contract between them which is an agreement to work towards specific changes in all three ego states. The first essential is that there is genuine motivation for change on the part of the child and the therapist and that this springs from an understanding, at a cognitive and feeling level, of the influences and experiences which are contributing to the child's concept of himself, and perhaps others, as losers who are not O.K. Once the old, rotten wood has been cut away the child can grow new shoots which are healthy and can be free to make new decisions about getting strokes, playing games, and living scripts.

SUMMARY

In this chapter there has been an attempt to examine, briefly, the major concepts of transactional analysis as a philosophy, personality theory, and treatment method, with special reference to staff working in a residential community. The basic optimism of T.A. as a tool for changing unhappy, unsuccessful personalities into 'winners' has been stressed and the importance for staff of understanding their own, as well as the child's ego-states, and transactions, stroke economy, psychological games, and scripts has been underlined. For a more detailed description of the theoretical basis of transactional analysis the reader is referred particularly to the works of Eric Berne, James and Jongeward, Woollams and Brown, and Thomas Harris. Suggestions for exercises and games to be used in T.A. group therapy in a residential community will be explored in Chapter 3.

# 3 Games and Exercises for Transactional Analysis Group Therapy

As T.A. is a method of looking at personality development and function which requires a fairly high cognitive involvement, the level at which a group therapy session can be pitched will depend to a large extent on the ability of the children in the group to think and to conceptualize. Residential therapists choosing to run group therapy on T.A. principles will need to master the basic principles of T.A. described in the previous chapter, then devise, in language appropriate to the age of the children in the group, ways of helping them to understand each principle. At the beginning of each of the following sets of exercises the basic principle is recalled briefly. The reader is referred to the relevant page in Chapter 2 where the principle is explained in more detail.

Alvyn and Margaret Freed (1973, 1976, 1977) have produced three excellent manuals aimed at explaining T.A. to three different age groups: *T.A. for Tots*, *T.A. for Kids*, and *T.A. for Teens*. Each of these books explains, in language appropriate to the age group, the major principles of T.A. and games and exercises are suggested. The books are colourfully and imaginatively illustrated and any residential therapist who wishes to do T.A. therapy would be well advised to consult them. Much of the language and illustrative material is, naturally, relevant to American culture and in this chapter I am to describe T.A. games and exercises geared to British children living in a residential community.

The exercises will be discussed under the following general headings:

Winners and losers
Ego states
Transactions
I'm O.K. You're O.K.
Strokes
Trading stamps
Games
Scripts
Contracts

The size of the group is preferably limited to a maximum of ten to ensure ease of interaction and, as T.A. is essentially to do with transactions, successful and unsuccessful, between children and children, parents and parents, parents and children, it is helpful if all the adults closely associated with the group of children can take part in the group therapy meetings. As with all group therapy, it is important to choose a room for the meetings which is warm, safe, and as neutral territory as possible so that all members of the group feel secure from interruption and at ease in the setting. As an introduction to the ideas of T.A., it is useful to start with the concept of 'Winners and losers' as this can be understood by all ages.

## WINNERS AND LOSERS

### Essential principle to be explained

Most children who find themselves in a residential community will feel that they are essentially some of life's losers. Often, through no fault of their own, they have been deprived of the basic degree of unconditional acceptance, love, security, and consistent management which most children receive as their birthright and they may well experience and express the feeling that they have been 'born to lose'.

The starting point for the T.A. therapist therefore is to convince the children that there are no 'born losers' but that everyone, whatever the odds, can become a winner. As their own experience up to that time may have made them highly sceptical of this possibility it is helpful to start the group therapy by discussing famous and successful people known to the children, who appeared to start life as 'losers'. The Beatles, for example, came from fairly deprived backgrounds and Winston Churchill was not a brilliant scholar in his youth. Nearer at home members of staff may be prepared to discuss the 'loser' feelings they had as children – exams failed, parental expectations not fulfilled, and to show how they have overcome these initial setbacks. The essential concept to convey to the children is that they are not entirely helpless in the face of unhappy experiences but that, with the help of the therapist and of their peer group, they can change their 'loser script' into a 'winner script'.

To many children, and adults, the concept of winning is usually winning at the expense of making someone else lose but this is not the sense in which T.A. uses the term. In T.A. terms winners are people who are not afraid to be themselves because they feel that they are O.K. and others are O.K. They are prepared to take responsibility for their own mistakes as well as to accept credit where it is due. They will be capable of making lasting friendships because they are trustworthy and able to consider others and their capacity to enjoy life will be tempered by their capacity to postpone enjoyment when necessary.

The following group exercises are useful in helping the children to think constructively about become a winner:

**Winning by others losing**

*Exercise One*

(a)  Divide the group into pairs.
(b)  Give one of each group five one penny pieces.
(c)  Ask them to toss each coin in turn while one of the partners calls 'Heads or Tails?'
(d)  Play this until one partner has won all or most of the coins.
(e)  Ask each player what it feels like to be (i) the loser and (ii) the winner.

*Exercise Two*

(a)  Stay with partner and keep one elbow on the table.

(b) Join hands with partner and hand wrestle by forcing the partner to touch the table with his hand.

(c) The partner who succeeds in doing this five times is the winner.

(d) Ask each player what it feels like to be (i) the loser and (ii) the winner.

## Winning by helping others to win

### Exercise One

(a) Give each member of the group five coins of a value high enough to be valuable, e.g. 10p.

(b) Explain to the group that each member in turn will be given the opportunity to give some or all of his coins away to other members of the group.

(c) Ask each member to do this.

(d) Observe which members give most freely.

(e) Ask each member how he felt when giving and receiving.

(f) Discuss the 'winner' feelings engendered by helping others and giving.

### Exercise Two

(a) Construct a simple obstacle course in the room, e.g. a chair to walk round, a table to crawl under, a pile of cushions to circumnavigate, a series of newspapers not to be trodden upon.

(b) Ask each child to choose a partner.

(c) Blindfold one of each couple in turn.

(d) Ask his partner to guide him successfully through the obstacle course.

(e) Time attempt and reward the winning blindfolded partner.

(f) Ask the guides how they felt when helping their partners to win.

## Recognizing winner and loser characteristics

### Exercise One

(a) Ask each group member to name the most important 'loser' and 'winner' characteristics of each of his parents.

(b) Of his houseparent and/or teacher.

*Exercise Two*

(1) Either as a group or individual exercise make up two collages of newspaper and magazine pictures, headlines and comments which represent (a) winners and winning and (b) losers and losing.

(2) With younger children read through a comic or fairy story picking out losers and winners.

## The importance of names

*Exercise One*

(1) Ask each member of the group in turn to say why he thought his parents gave him his particular name and whether he feels it to be a 'winner' or 'loser' name and what characteristics the name implies. This may highlight the feeling, for example, that the parents wanted a child of the opposite sex and so gave the child a unisex name, like Leslie or Jo, or the name may seem particularly babyish, like Robin, or very adult, like George, or represent a happy characteristic, like Joy or Felicity.

(2) Ask each member of the group what name he would choose for himself and why.

EGO STATES (Page 31)

## Essential principle to be explained

The difficulty in talking to children about the three ego states of Parent, Adult, Child, is that since they are still children they will assume that they are always using their Child Ego and that this is always appropriate. A starting point for explaining the ego states is to ask each member of the group to write or talk about his own behaviour under the following three headings:

(1) I should . . .
(2) I think . . .
(3) I want . . .

The therapist then goes on to illustrate, from the lists provided, that the 'I should' suggestions are likely to have been inspired by the injunctions and permissions of parental authority figures, that the 'I think' suggestions are the child using his Adult or Little Professor and that the 'I want' suggestions will come from his Child. Using visual aids (see Chapter 2 pages 34—40) the therapist helps the children to understand that both adults and children can be acting from any one of the three ego states at any given moment.

### Exercise One

(1) Ask the group to describe an incident in which children had been in trouble in the residential community, e.g. two houseparents one night, well after bed-time, discover three children raiding the kitchen and taking biscuits and cakes.

(2) Ask children from the group to play the roles of the children and the houseparents and to act the scene, each actor choosing a different ego state from which to respond. For instance, the scene could be enacted thus:

*First Houseparent*
  'You naughty children, how dare you get out of bed after lights out and come to steal food from the kitchen?' (Critical Parent)

*First Child*
  'I'm very sorry, I expect we'll have to go to bed early now for at least a week!' (Adapted Child)

*Second Child*
  'It's not fair! We always have to go to bed early and we're not stealing — it's not your food anyway!' (Free Child)

*Second Houseparent*
  'Come along, into bed quickly before you catch cold — you've nothing on your feet and you've already got a cough, Marcia.' (Nurturing Parent)

*Third Child*
  'I suppose the best thing we can do now is to apologize, put the food back and get into bed quickly and promise not to do this again.' (Adult)

**Parent ego exercises**

*Aim* – To help the children in the group to become aware of which parts of their own personality have sprung directly, or indirectly, from parents and parent figures and to be able to reject these without guilt if they are not constructive attitudes or behaviours.

*Exercise One*

(1) Make a list of subjects about which the group thinks parents usually have strong feelings, e.g.:
> education
> choosing a job
> religion
> the government
> drugs
> smoking
> sex
> money

(2) Ask each member of the group to say what attitude he thinks each of his parents would hold about each subject and if he himself holds similar attitudes.

*Exercise Two*

(1) Each member of the group chooses a partner and spends five minutes discussing with him how each of his parents would describe him.
(2) After repeating the exercise so that each partner has given the descriptions, ask each child which parts of the descriptions he agrees are correct about him.

**Child ego exercises**

*Aim* – To help the children in the group to understand that their child ego will be with them throughout life and that it is the part of the personality which can give the most pleasure but also the most pain.

*Exercise One*

(1) Ask each of the group to think about a younger child whom he knows well — perhaps a brother or sister or neighbour's child.

(2) Ask each of the group to describe the child's behaviour: (a) when he is having harmless fun, e.g. when he is playing with sand and water; (b) when he is having destructive fun, e.g. breaking toys or taking another child's toys; (c) when he can be seen to be adapting to his parents, e.g. trying to eat like a grown up, doing as he is told when he clearly would prefer to be doing something else; (d) when he has worked something out for himself, e.g. 'If I go to bed as soon as mummy tells me to she will read me a long story'.

(3) Talk over the concepts of Free Child, Adapted Child, and Little Professor with the group using the illustrations they have provided.

*Exercise Two: Games for the Free Child*

(1) Each member of the group has a large piece of paper on which he paints (a) with his fingers and (b) with his feet. This is clearly a messy game but guaranteed to let out the Free Child!

(2) Each member of the group is given a tray containing clay, sand, and a container of water, plus any other available play materials, e.g. foam rubber, cardboard, bricks, and is asked to use these materials to build an imaginary 'home' or 'world'.

*Exercise Three: Games for the Adapted Child*

(1) Ask each member of the group to look back over the previous week and give an example of when he felt he adapted to the demands of the adult closest to him emotionally, e.g. own parent, houseparent, or teacher.

(2) Discuss with the group the rules which exist in their residential community and try to determine where they are clearly designed to encourage the children to adapt to the needs of the staff and where they are more for the benefit of the children or the group as a whole.

*Exercise Four*

(1) Describe to the group a problematic situation which might occur within the residential community, e.g. there are two rival television programmes on different channels and half the group wishes to watch one but the other half of the group wishes to watch the other.

(2) Ask the group to use their Little Professors to work out the best solution to the problem.

## Adult ego exercises

*Aim* — To help the children to understand that, although in age they are still children, they can develop a growing capacity to think for themselves and to make decisions based on a sound knowledge of facts and uncontaminated by unhelpful Child and Parent influences; to value education in its widest sense to include knowledge of self and others as well as formal lesson subjects.

*Exercise One*

(1) Choose topics which are of interest to the group and liable to be controversial, e.g. coloured people, God, sex, policemen.

(2) Under each heading collect spontaneous opinions from each of the group and write them on a blackboard.

(3) Go over the opinions with the group and divide them into opinions based on (a) prejudice, (b) fantasy, and (c) a knowledge of the facts.

(4) Help the group to see where their prejudices might spring from and to review their own prejudices and fantasies.

TRANSACTIONS (page 35)

## Essential principle to be explained

Children in a residential community are forced to relate to more people in the course of an average day than most children because they are living in a group of children much larger than in any family and are relating to far more adults and authority/parent figures than their contemporaries who live in their own home. Because of the nature of the network of relationships which has led to placement in such a community, they are more likely to have difficulty in making satisfactory complementary transactions through lack of experience in trusting relationships. It is important, therefore, that children in a T.A. therapy group should be helped to recognize the type of transactions, crossed and ulterior, which they have grown accustomed to make in the absence of complementary transactions and that the possibility of making trusting and friendly transactions with peers and adults should be explored.

*Exercise One: 'What do you say after you say, "Hello"?'*

(1) Ask each member of the group to choose a partner.
(2) Each partner in turn greets his partner with 'Hello' followed by a question, e.g. 'How do you feel today?'
(3) The partner gives a spontaneous reply, e.g. 'Fine, thank you, how do you feel?' (complementary transaction) or 'Why do you want to know, it's none of your business?' (crossed transaction) or 'I'm O.K.', said with a frown which belies the reply (ulterior transaction).
(4) Ask the rest of the group to identify the type of transaction which has taken place.

*Exercise Two*

(1) Ask each member of the group to design a tee-shirt motto for himself which he writes on a large piece of paper and pins onto his back, e.g. 'I rule O.K.' or 'I'm a handsome fellow' or 'Nobody loves me'.
(2) Give each of the group a pencil and tell them to put either a tick against the message on each of the other tee-shirts if they feel that the motto gives a true message about the wearer or a cross if the message does not ring true.
(3) Ask each person to remove the paper from his back and count the number of ticks and crosses he has been given.
(4) Discuss how people give out ulterior messages by what they say about themselves or how they behave.

*Exercise Three*

Discuss some of the most popular television commercials and try to spot the ulterior messages which are being conveyed, e.g. advertisements for beauty preparations which imply that if a woman is not young or beautiful she cannot be lovable, or those which imply that if a mother does not use a certain washing powder she is a bad mother and wife.

I'M O.K. YOU'RE O.K. (page 44)

**Essential principle to be explained**

Reverting back to the principle of 'Winners and Losers', winners, in T.A. terms, are people who feel happy with themselves and the way they are and also with the way other people are. To be O.K. is to accept yourself realistically, to be proud of your achievements and 'good' qualities and to take responsibility for your faults and shortcomings instead of blaming them on others. To see others as O.K. is to accept them realistically and as people worthy of respect and consideration. Although many children in a residential community will feel that they, and/or others, are not O.K., this can change to produce a happier outlook on life.

*Exercise One*

(1) Having discussed the concept of 'O.K.' with the group, draw the life-position diagram on a board: see *Figure 3(1)*.

*Figure 3(1)* Possible psychological life positions

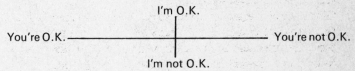

(2) Ask each member of the group to say in which quarter they would place themselves at that moment in time, e.g. 'I'm O.K. – You're not O.K.' in relation to the rest of the group.
(3) Ask each member to say which is their favourite position when they feel under attack from someone or some situation, giving an example from something which has happened to them in the past week.

*Exercise Two*

(1) Construct a self-rating questionnaire for each member of
the group providing a range of 1–10 points: see *Figure 3(2)*.

*Figure 3(2)* Self-rating questionnaire

| How O.K. do I feel about – | 1 | 2 | 3 | 4 | 5 | 6 | 7 | 8 | 9 | 10 |
|---|---|---|---|---|---|---|---|---|---|---|
| myself as a person | | | | | | | | | | |
| my family | | | | | | | | | | |
| school | | | | | | | | | | |
| my residential community | | | | | | | | | | |
| being a boy/girl | | | | | | | | | | |
| being young and dependent | | | | | | | | | | |
| how I look | | | | | | | | | | |
| being part of this group | | | | | | | | | | |

Total

(2) Ask each member to put ticks in the appropriate boxes and
to arrive at a grand total out of a possible 80.
(3) Encourage the group to discuss any very low scores to see
how they might be improved.


STROKES (page 43)

**Essential principle to be explained**

Just as babies need to be held and cuddled and experience close
physical contact with the people caring for them, the developing
personality needs to receive an abundant supply of psychological stroking in order to grow into a healthy, well-balanced
personality. If babies are not given physical stroking they lose
the will to live and through refusing food they lose the ability to
digest food and make use of it when it is given. If the personality
is not given the positive psychological strokes it needs for
growth, it will seek negative strokes as a better alternative to no
strokes at all and will gradually lose the ability to 'digest'
positive strokes when they are given.

Alvyn and Margaret Freed (1977:8) describe a stroke as 'any sort of act by someone else that lets you know they are there: a smile, pat on the back, a whistle, voice, anything like that. . . . What we say and the way we look at each other as well as the way we touch each other can all be pleasant strokes.'

As many of the children in the group will have learnt to survive by receiving, then learning to seek, negative strokes as the only strokes available, the T.A. principle of giving, receiving, and asking for positive strokes will not be an easy one for them to accept. In my experience, however, it is one of the most therapeutically useful principles contained in T.A. and it is well worth spending time on it in group therapy sessions.

Steiner (1971) christened positive strokes 'Warm Fuzzies' and negative strokes 'Cold Pricklies' and it is useful to start group therapy, which is to explore the concept of 'strokes', by reading the story he has written to illustrate his Fuzzy concept.

## A Fuzzytale − by Claude M. Steiner, Ph.D.

Once upon a time, a long time ago, there lived two very happy people called Tim and Maggie with two children called John and Lucy. To understand how happy they were, you have to understand how things were in those days. You see, in those happy days everyone was given at birth a small, soft, Fuzzy Bag. Any time a person reached into this bag he was able to pull out a Warm Fuzzy. Warm Fuzzies were very much in demand because whenever somebody was given a Warm Fuzzy it made him feel warm and fuzzy all over. People who didn't get Warm Fuzzies regularly were in danger of developing a sickness in their back which caused them to shrivel up and die.

In those days it was very easy to get Warm Fuzzies. Any time that somebody felt like it, he might walk up to you and say, 'I'd like to have a Warm Fuzzy.' You would then reach into your bag and pull out a Fuzzy the size of a little girl's hand. As soon as the Fuzzy saw the light of day it would smile and blossom into a large, shaggy Warm Fuzzy. You then would lay it on the person's shoulder or head or lap and it would snuggle up and melt right against their skin and make them feel good all over.

People were always asking each other for Warm Fuzzies, and since they were always given freely, getting enough of them was never a problem. There were always plenty to go around and as a consequence everyone was happy and felt warm and fuzzy most of the time.

One day a bad witch became angry because everyone was so happy and no one was buying her potions and salves. This witch was very clever and she devised a very wicked plan. One beautiful morning she crept up to Tim while Maggie was playing with their daughter and whispered in his ear, 'See here, Tim, look at all the Fuzzies that Maggie is giving to Lucy: You know, if she keeps it up, eventually she is going to run out and then there won't be any left for you.'

Tim was astonished. He turned to the witch and said, 'Do you mean to tell me that there isn't a Warm Fuzzy in our bag every time we reach into it?'

And the witch said, 'No, absolutely not, and once you run out, that's it. You don't have any more.' With this, she flew away on her broom, laughing and cackling hysterically.

Tim took this to heart and began to notice every time Maggie gave up a Warm Fuzzy to someone else. Eventually he got very worried and upset because he liked Maggie's Warm Fuzzies very much and did not want to give them up. He certainly did not think it was right for Maggie to be spending all her Warm Fuzzies on the children and on other people. He began to complain every time he saw Maggie giving a Warm Fuzzy to somebody else, and because Maggie liked him very much, she stopped giving Warm Fuzzies to other people as often, and reserved them for him.

The children watched this and soon began to get the idea that it was wrong to give up Warm Fuzzies any time you were asked or felt like it. They, too, became very careful. They would watch their parents closely and whenever they felt that one of their parents was giving too many Fuzzies to others, they also began to object. They began to feel worried whenever they gave away too many Warm Fuzzies. Even though they found a Warm Fuzzy every time they reached into their bag, they reached in less and less and became more and more stingy. Soon people began to notice the lack of Warm Fuzzies, and they began to feel less and less fuzzy. They began to shrivel up and occasionally, people would die from lack of Warm Fuzzies. More and more people went to the witch to buy her potions and salves even though they didn't seem to work.

Well, the situation was getting very serious indeed. The bad witch, who had been watching all of this, didn't really want the people to die, so she devised a new plan. She gave everyone a bag that was very similar to the Fuzzy Bag except that this one was cold while the Fuzzy Bag was warm. Inside of the witch's bag were Cold Pricklies. Cold Pricklies did not make people feel warm and fuzzy, but made them feel cold and prickly instead. But, they did prevent people's backs from shriveling up. So, from then on, every time somebody said, 'I want a Warm Fuzzy,' people who were worried about depleting their supply would say, 'I can't give you a Warm Fuzzy, but would you like a Cold Prickly?' Sometimes, two people would walk up to each other, thinking they could get a Warm Fuzzy, but one or the other of them would change his mind and they would wind up giving each other Cold Pricklies. So, the end result was that while very few people were dying, a lot of people were still unhappy and feeling very cold and prickly.

The situation got very complicated because, since the coming of the witch, there were less and less Warm Fuzzies around, so Warm Fuzzies, which used to be thought of as free as air, became extremely valuable. This caused people to do all sorts of things in order to obtain them. Before the witch had appeared, people used to gather in groups of three or four or five, never caring too much who was giving Warm Fuzzies to whom. After the coming of the witch, people began to pair off and to reserve all their Warm Fuzzies for each other exclusively. If ever one of the two persons forgot himself and gave a Warm Fuzzy to someone else, he would immediately feel guilty about it because he knew his partner would probably resent the loss of a Warm Fuzzy. People who could not find a generous partner had to buy their Warm Fuzzies and had to work long hours to earn the money. Another thing which happened was that some people would take Cold Pricklies — which were limitless and freely available − coat them white and fuzzy and pass them on as Warm Fuzzies. These counterfeit Warm Fuzzies were really Plastic Fuzzies, and they caused additional difficulties. For instance, two people would get together and freely exchange Plastic Fuzzies, which presumably should make them feel good, but they came away feeling bad instead. Since they thought they had been exchanging Warm Fuzzies, people grew very confused about this, never realizing that their cold prickly feelings were really the result of the fact that they had been given a lot of Plastic Fuzzies.

So, the situation was very, very dismal and it all started because of the coming of the witch who made people believe that some day, when least expected, they might reach into their Warm Fuzzy Bag and find no more.

Not long ago a young woman with big hips, born under the sign of Aquarius, came to this unhappy land. She had not heard about the bad witch and was not worried about running out of Warm Fuzzies. She gave them out freely, even when not asked. They called her the Hip Woman and disapproved of her because she was giving the children the idea that they should not worry about running out of Warm Fuzzies. The children liked her very much because they felt good around her and they, too, began to give out Warm Fuzzies whenever they felt like it. The grown-ups became concerned and decided to pass a law to protect the children from depleting their supplies of Warm Fuzzies. The law made it a criminal offense to give out Warm Fuzzies in a reckless manner. The children, however, seemed not to care and in spite of the law, they continued to give each other Warm Fuzzies whenever they felt like it and always when asked. Because there were many, many children, almost as many as grown-ups, it began to look as if maybe they would have their way.

As of now it is hard to say what will happen. Will the grown-up forces of law and order stop the recklessness of the children? Are the grown-ups going to join with the Hip Woman and the children in taking a chance that there will always be as many Warm Fuzzies as needed? Will they re-member the days their children are trying to bring back when

Warm Fuzzies were abundant because people gave them away freely?

One of the most difficult habits for children and staff alike in a residential community to acquire is that of giving positive strokes, or Warm Fuzzies, freely. It is always easy to comment on bad behaviour i.e. give a cold prickly to a child who is doing something wrong, but if he is behaving as he should this will go without comment. It is useful, therefore, to start each group session with an opportunity for staff and children to give warm fuzzies to each other in the shape of positive comments, votes of thanks, kind observations. In my own residential community we start each day with a short 'Warm Fuzzy session' and it is interesting to observe how children who have formerly been spiteful and hurtful towards their peers gradually realize that not only do they give pleasure to others by giving Warm Fuzzies but, through giving, they also receive a feeling of warmth themselves.

If the children have grasped the principle of the three ego states − Parent, Adult, Child − discuss with them the need for each of the ego states to receive strokes. The following exercises will help the group to understand the principle of 'strokes' and, I have found, the children will start to create new games and exercises around this theme for themselves.

*Exercise One*

(1) Ask each member of the group to say what he thinks is the favourite positive stroke he gives to (a) his mother, (b) his father, (c) his houseparent or teacher.
(2) Ask each member of the group to say what he thinks is the most common negative stroke that he gives to these important adults.

*Exercise Two*

(1) Ask each member of the group to describe something that has happened to him that day which made him feel not O.K.

(2) Get the group to make suggestions as to what positive stroke someone could have given to make him feel O.K. again.

### Exercise Three

Ask each member of the group to describe (a) one positive stroke he has given that day, (b) one situation in which he received a positive stroke, (c) one situation in which he asked for a positive stroke.

### Exercise Four

(1) Using pieces of brightly coloured fur fabric, e.g. orange or red, show each child how to make a Warm Fuzzy, using pieces of black and white felt, to create a smile. See *Figure 3(3)*.

*Figure 3(3)* Warm Fuzzy

(2) Using any materials which seem appropriate, e.g. tin foil, cold-coloured paper and card, ask each child to make a Cold Prickly.

### Exercise Five

Give each child a large piece of paper and paints or coloured pencils and ask him to design a Warm Fuzzy poster. The one I have on my wall depicts a huge, smiling Warm Fuzzy, who is saying, 'Have a Nice Day!'

*Exercise Six*

(1) Pin a sheet of paper onto the back of each member of the group.
(2) Ask each person to write something positive on every other person's piece of paper.
(3) To show the importance of being able to accept gracefully positive strokes when they are given, ask each person to read out his list in a tone of voice and a manner which is accepting and unashamed of the compliments he has been given.

TRADING.STAMPS (page 46)

**Essential principle to be explained**

In T.A. terms psychological trading stamps are the favourite feelings, good and bad, that a person has learnt to collect from early in his childhood. They are called trading stamps because, like Green Shield or Co-op stamps, once the owner has a sufficiently large collection of stamps he can cash them in for a prize. His brown, or negative stamps, coming from favourite feelings, such as anger, guilt, suspicion, rejection, stupidity, will be saved up and cashed in eventually to justify a piece of negative behaviour, e.g. an aggressive outburst, a depression, an illness, stealing and, in extreme cases, suicide or murder. His gold, or positive stamps, coming from favourite feelings, such as being successful, helpful, thoughtful of others, skilled, interesting, will be cashed in for treats like buying new clothes, going out for a meal, going to bed later than usual, having fun.

People who collect good feelings about themselves are more easily able to help others to feel good and, through feeling that they and others are O.K., become winners. People who collect bad feelings tend to provoke others into responding badly to them and so their brown-stamp collection keeps growing and they become losers.

One aspect of T.A. therapy is to help the child to give up collecting brown stamps and to enable him to become a winner.

*Exercise One*

(1) Read the following story to the group.

Joan was not a very popular girl at school because the other children found her very moody and not much fun to have around. She looked as though she didn't care about this but in reality she felt hurt when nobody chose her for their rounders team or wanted to sit next to her in class. At least once every few weeks the feelings of resentment she had stored up would produce a bad headache or an upset tummy and she would refuse to go to school for a day.

Her sister, Helen, was just the opposite, which made life even more difficult for Joan. Somehow nice things just seemed to happen naturally to Helen and she always had friends and was chosen by teachers to take part in special activities. As Helen was confident and happy in herself, she was able to make others happy and in this way she stored up feelings of being O.K. Every few weeks she would treat herself to a new record or would give a party and she was able to look forward to doing well when she left school and went to University.

(2) Ask the group to decide which kind of feelings Joan collected and how she might have learnt to collect these feelings.

(3) Ask the same questions about Helen.

(4) Ask for suggestions for ways in which Joan could start to collect gold instead of brown stamps.

*Exercise Two*

(1) Ask each member of the group to describe an angry or hurt feeling he has had that day but done nothing about, e.g. after he had been punished for something he didn't do or had received a bad mark for a piece of school work which he thought he had done well.

(2) Collect suggestions from the group as to what each child could do to prevent the bad feeling being stored away as a brown stamp.

GAMES (page 47)

**Essential principle to be explained**

In the usual sense of the word, games are either a way of relaxing and having fun with friends or providing an outlet for competitive drives which produce a winner and a loser. In T.A. terms games are tried and true ways of getting strokes, either positive or negative, when the player does not feel he is going to get them just for being himself. The strokes obtained through games, however, are never really satisfying as they are not based on an 'I'm O.K. You're O.K.' life position. T.A. therapy aims to help people to recognize the games they play and to seek alternative and more satisfactory ways in which to obtain positive strokes. A person who plays T.A. games regularly is likely to choose one of three common roles: Victim, Persecutor, or Rescuer. These roles were chosen in negative early childhood experience and are not responses to present situations. A T.A. game is played over and over again with a predictable course of moves which always lead to a negative pay-off in which one or both of the players feel not O.K. The transactions which take place in a Game are always Ulterior but both players are in collusion with this.

## Exercise One

(1) Having explained the nature of T.A. games to the group, tell them that each person is going to try to identify his own favourite game through answering the following questions contained in the James and Jongeward Game Plan (1975:134). Specimen answers are given below.
   (a) 'What keeps happening over and over that leaves some-one feeling bad?
   (b) How does it start?
   (c) What happens next?
   (d) How does it end?
   (e) How does each person feel when it ends?'

   (a) Jane is always getting into trouble with her house-mother for being cheeky but she believes she is just telling the truth.
   (b) The housemother asks Jane to do the washing up. Jane argues that it is not her turn and swears at the house-mother.
   (c) The housemother reacts from her Child and shouts and

loses her temper with Jane, sending her to bed straight-away.

(d) Jane stamps off in a temper tantrum and the house-mother drops a plate.

(e) Jane feels that, although she has received strokes in terms of attention, these are very negative strokes which leave her feeling rejected.

The housemother feels she has lost the game because she lost her temper in front of the other children and that she wished she could have handled the situation more positively.

(2) Discuss with the group how each of the 'unhappy endings' could be avoided.

*Exercise Two*

(1) Ask the children to select a scene from life in their residential community which seems to happen over and over again, e.g. Terence, in order to obtain the steady supply of strokes, negative or positive, which he craves picks a fight with Peter, a boy much smaller than he. Peter runs to his favourite housemother and tells tales about Terence, omitting to inform her that he had somewhat provoked the attack by calling Terence names. The housemother, who has a soft spot for Peter and likes to keep him close to her and extremely dependent, punishes Terence without looking into the matter further.

(2) Ask the children to role play this situation, identifying the roles of Victim, Persecutor, Rescuer.

(3) Suggest ways in which this could be prevented from turning into a T.A. game.

*Exercise Three*

Ask the group to describe games from their own experience which are designed:

(a) to collect put-downs, e.g. deliberate breaking of rules to be found out and punished (Victim games).

(b) to put others down, e.g. telling tales to get others into trouble (Persecutor games).

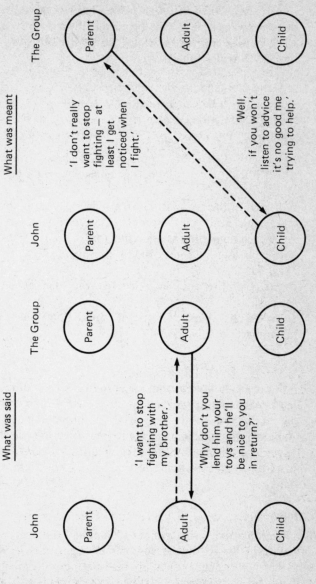

*Figure 3(4)* 'Yes – but' transactions

What was said

John      The Group

Parent      Parent

Adult      Adult

'I want to stop fighting with my brother.'

'Why don't you lend him your toys and he'll be nice to you in return?'

Child      Child

What was meant

John      The Group

Parent      Parent

Adult      Adult

'I don't really want to stop fighting – at least I get noticed when I fight.'

Child      Child

'Well, if you won't listen to advice it's no good me trying to help.'

(c) to offer help when the other person has not asked for and does not want it, e.g. telling someone the answer to a sum when he was enjoying working the answer out slowly for himself (Rescuer games).

## Exercises to illustrate some common T.A. games

### Exercise Four: The 'Yes, but' game

(1) Ask one of the children to present to the group something which is a problem to him, e.g. quarrelling with brothers and sisters.
(2) Ask each of the group to make a suggestion as to how the child could deal with the problem.
(3) After each suggestion ask the child to give a reason why that particular solution is no good by starting the sentence with 'Yes, but. . . .'
(4) Discuss with the group how they felt when their advice was rejected.
(5) Draw on the board the type of transactions which have taken place, see *Figure 3(4)*.

### Exercise Five: Wooden Leg game

(1) Ask the group members to name someone they know who has a real handicap which he seems to be able to overcome, e.g. not having a father.
(2) Ask the group members to name something they do themselves to get sympathy and attention through an imaginary handicap, e.g. pretending to find school work impossibly hard.

### Exercise Six

Ask the group to describe games of 'Cops and Robbers' which take place in the residential community, i.e. games in which rules are deliberately broken so that the player can attract positive strokes from his peers if he succeeds and is not caught and negative strokes from staff if he is found out.

*Exercise Seven*

To illustrate the T.A. game of 'Uproar', which often takes place in a residential community, ask each member of the group to choose a partner with whom he will role play for the rest of the group a situation in which each partner criticizes the other partner in turn until the game ends in them both stamping away with feelings of 'I'm O.K. He's not O.K.'

SCRIPTS (page 55)

## Essential principle to be explained

The T.A. concept of life scripts brings us back to our starting point of Winners and Losers. When people talk about fate or say things like 'It must be meant' or 'It's bound to happen to me' they are implying that their life is pre-ordained like the script of a play or story and that there is very little they can do about it. T.A. therapy aims to help the individual to see that his life is not totally determined by outside forces but that he is capable, with insight into his own 'script' and with help from new relationships and experiences, to influence considerably the course of his own life.

As most children who live in a residential community feel that they are on a loser script, the ability to re-write their own scripts is of vital importance. The starting point from which to plan a new script is an understanding of the present one and of the influences which created it. The following exercises are designed to help this understanding.

*Exercise One*

(1) Discuss the importance of families and the expectations of what each child will do and become as conveyed through family sayings.
(2) Ask each child to give one saying about himself from his family, e.g.:
  'He's going to be good with his hands.'
  'He'll never do anything with his lack of brains!'
  'If he goes on like he is he'll come to no good!'

*Figure 3(5)* Family tree

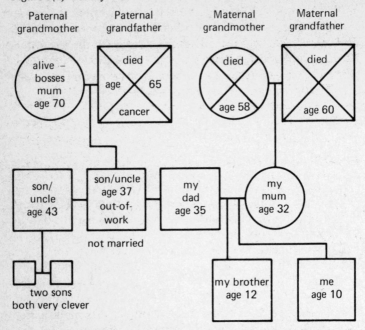

'He's going to be the clever one in the family.'
(3) Ask each member of the group to give one 'loser' and one 'winner' message that he gets from his family.

## Exercise Two

In order to assess how a child perceives his family so that he can describe more clearly to himself and to his therapist where he fits into his family system, it can be helpful to plot, with the child, what he knows of his own heritage. This would probably start with his grandparents, maternal and paternal, and the therapist would elicit significant information about the personality and influence on other family members of each relative (see *Figure 3(5)*).

## Exercise Three

(1) Discuss the importance of cultural influences on scripts under the following headings:

    (a) race and colour
    (b) religion
    (c) politics
    (d) working-class and middle-class cultures

(2) Ask each member of the group to name one family tradition which it would be very hard to break, e.g. father never washes up, mother does not go to the pub without father, grandparent's advice is always or never taken.

(3) Ask each member of the group to name one tradition from the town or district in which he lives that has been handed down from generation to generation, e.g. in a mining area, the men and women tend to go out socially with their own sex, people in Scotland think that New Year is more important than Christmas, mill towns close down for the same two weeks each year, even when the mills themselves are no longer in action. These are sub-cultural influences on scripts.

## Exercise Four

(1) Discuss with the group the expectations which arise from the stereotyping of male and female roles and behaviours.

(2) Ask each child to complete the following sentences:
    Girls are....
    Boys are....
    Men are....
    Women are....
    Fathers are....
    Mothers are....
    Daughters are....
    Sons are....

(3) Repeat the exercise with sentences beginning:
    Girls can do....
    Boys can do ... etc.

(4) Repeat the exercise with sentences beginning:
    Girls cannot do....
    Boys cannot do ... etc.

*Exercise Five*

(1) Discuss some well-known fairy stories in terms of life
    scripts picking out the winner and loser characters, e.g.:
    Cinderella, who changed from a loser to a winner.
    Peter Pan, who never wanted to grow up.
    The Princess and the Frog, the frog who is unable to be
    handsome without someone else's help.
(2) Ask each member of the group to say with which fairy story
    character he identifies and discuss the implications of this
    for his life script, e.g. does he perceive his life script as a
    tragedy, a comedy or just rather ordinary and boring?
(3) Ask each member of the group to make up a modern fairy
    tale with himself as the hero succeeding in changing from a
    loser to a winner.

*Exercise Six*

Ask each member of the group to think about his own life and
to give, in story form, with himself as the central character, an
account of his life:

(a) as it was five years ago;
(b) as it is now;
(c) as he hopes it will be in ten years' time.


CONTRACTS

**Essential principle to be explained**

All members of a therapy group should be there, ideally,
because they wish to bring about some change in the way they
think, feel, behave in relation to or are treated by other people.
It is sometimes difficult to get away from the feeling of being in
a captive, as opposed to a voluntary, group when one lives in a
residential community but unless there is some commitment to
the desire for change within members of the group, the therapy
is highly unlikely to be successful.

I have left discussion of contracts for change until the end of
this chapter although, on the face of it, making a contract for
change in group therapy might logically come at the beginning of

therapy. Until the group member, however, has gained some insight into what he thinks and feels and how he behaves and why, he can have no clear idea of what changes he wishes to make.

Once the group has achieved a minimum level of insight through discussion and some of the exercises previously described, it is possible to draw up contracts for change with individuals in the group and the group as a whole.

James and Jongeward (1975:182) define a T.A. contract as follows:

> 'A contract for change is a specific goal that a person decides to accomplish and a carefully thought out plan to reach that goal. It is an Adult commitment to one's self and/or to someone else to make a change. Usually contracts are a move away from the negative aspects in one's life to establishing more positive aspects.
>
> The contract must be clear, concise and direct. It involves:
> (1) a decision to work on a specific problem.
> (2) a statement of the precise goal to be reached, put in language that is simple enough for the inner Child to understand.
> (3) the possibility of the goal's being fulfilled; it must be realistic.'

The following exercises may be useful in helping each individual in the group to draw up a realistic contract for change which can be monitored and evaluated by the group as the therapy sessions proceed.

*Exercise One*

(1) Explain to the group that merely wishing to change is not enough as it involves no real commitment but deals with a problem at the fantasy level.
(2) Ask each member of the group to explain the problem he wishes to work on, e.g. being violent and aggressive with other children, to the group and then to complete the following statements:

I wish or would like to do....

I am making a decision to do....

My actions this week will be....

*Exercise Two*

(1) Explain to the group that it is easier and more encouraging to choose small, achievable goals for change early in therapy as this will build up one's confidence in the possibility of change.

(2) Ask each member of the group to draw up a hierarchical list of four change goals, starting with a very simple one and finishing with the most difficult, e.g.:

    (a) Getting up in the morning as soon as I am told.

    (b) Not aggravating others at breakfast time.

    (c) Doing as I am told without argument.

    (d) Not losing my temper all day.

*Exercise Three: putting the problem into a smaller frame*

(1) Ask each member of the group in turn to describe the biggest change he would like to take place in his life, e.g. he would like to be friends with everyone in the residential community and to gain the approval of all the staff.

(2) Ask the group to suggest ways in which the minimum change in this area could be achieved, e.g. that he chooses one child with whom he will definitely not squabble that day.

*Exercise Four: putting the problem into a larger frame*

(1) Draw the diagram in *Figure 3(6a)* on a board.

(2) Ask the group to join the dots with a piece of chalk using only four lines and never allowing the chalk to leave the board.

(3) Show them the solution which is to go right outside the existing frame: see *Figure 3(6b)*.

(4) Ask someone to describe a problem with which he wishes to deal, e.g. getting on better with his parents.

(5) Collect suggestions for how the problem might be solved by putting it into a larger frame, e.g. looking at the role, helpful or unhelpful, that the grandparents might play in the family.

*Exercise Five*

Having asked each member of the group, with the help of group discussion, to select a change goal, he is prepared to set for

given to them but not when a bell was rung. To
ning experience a bell was rung immediately
s given on a number of occasions. After this, the
without any presentation of food was enough to
ion. Learning through this type of experience is
gh responses being evoked by new stimuli.

and experiments with human subjects proved
ally possible to condition some human responses
nethod. In a somewhat heartless experiment
yner (1920) established a fear of white rats in a
ert, who originally had no fear of the rats and
with them. He was, however, afraid of loud
eriments sounded a loud gong on several occa-
ert was playing with a rat, after which Albert
ved signs of fear when the rat was presented to
ugh the gong was not sounded.

given to the two types of stimuli and the two types
were: (a) 'unconditioned stimulus' and 'uncon-
ponse'; and (b) 'conditioned stimulus' and 'con-
sponse'. The 'unconditioned stimulus' was, in the
vlov's dogs, the presentation of food followed by the
ioned response', salivation; the 'conditioned
was the bell followed by the 'conditioned response' of
n.

xtent to which a new and neutral stimulus, e.g. the bell,
conditioned to evoke a response is governed by the
of the presentation in relation to the unconditioned
s, i.e. the food. It was found that the new stimulus must
nted before the unconditioned stimulus, the food, was
d for response to the new stimulus to be established.

a residential community, therefore, we wish to elicit
w piece of desirable behaviour through the use of clas-
nditioning techniques, it is essential to present the new
stimulus just before the existing unconditioned
is. For example, meal times in a residential community
e preceded by noisy and disruptive behaviour which
when the food is actually put in front of the children and
begins. If a member of staff wishes to produce an

*Figure 3(6a)* Joining dots – problem

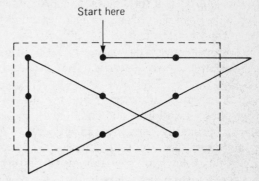

*Figure 3(6b)* Joining dots – solution

himself, draw up, in writing, individual contracts within the
following frame:

What do I need to do...?
What am I willing to do...?
Whom can I ask for help...?
Whom do I trust to measure my progress...?

SUMMARY

In this chapter it was assumed that the reader had understood and
familiarized himself with the theories of Transactional Analysis
described in the previous chapter. Each of the major principles of
T.A. as a therapy was examined in the light of group exercises
which would enable members of a therapy group to be helped by
that principle. Above all the T.A. belief that it is possible to
change one's self-image from 'not O.K.' to 'O.K.' and one's life
script from a 'loser script' to a 'winner script' was stressed.

# 4 The Behaviourist Approach

## INTRODUCTION

There are similarities between the behaviourist approach to therapy and the approach of the Transactional Analysts in that each believes in the possibility of change and each employs techniques which concentrate on working with the positive, or potentially positive, aspects of a personality. The major difference between the two theoretical standpoints is that, whereas the T.A. therapist is helping the child through his own awareness of the negative influences of his previous experience and an insight into his attitudes and emotional responses, the behaviourist is primarily interested in present observable behaviour and does not think it important to trace the antecedents of this behaviour or to gain insight into thoughts and feelings for changes in behaviour to take place. Behaviour therapists base their methods on principles derived from learning theory.

Learning, in the behaviourist sense of the word, can be defined as a relatively permanent change in behaviour which occurs as a result of prior experience, although the change may not be apparent until a situation arises in which the new learning can be demonstrated. Learning, therefore, is a change in behaviour *potential* and is one way of describing what we are hoping to achieve with the children who live in our residential communities. Many of them come to us with an unhelpful and self-destructive set of learnt behaviours, such as going into each new experience aggressively or even violently or, at the other extreme, tending to withdraw into an inner world or shell when under some real or imagined threat. Whatever therapeutic intervention we employ, no matter what the theoretical basis for our methods, it is this potential for relatively permanent change in

behaviour which we see as the goal of treatment ficient for us to help a child to be able to adjust h a way which he can achieve within the comparati residential community. He must also be able to learnt acceptable behaviour to situations outside such as home and school.

The two major approaches to treatment which from learning theory are (1) behaviour modifica the work of psychologists, led by Skinner, and e niques of operant conditioning, often throug token economy; (2) behaviour therapy, derived the work of psychologists, Wolpe and Lazarus, techniques of systematic desensitization. In orde relevance and potential value of such techniques group therapists, the major concepts of learning discussed under the following headings:

Classical Conditioning
Operant Conditioning:
    Through Positive Reinforcement
    Through Negative Reinforcement and Punishmen
    Through Extinction
Modelling
Counter-Conditioning and Systematic Desensitization

The important point to bear in mind when planning a ment strategy which aims primarily at changing behavi precursor to a change in attitude or feeling is that there a two major types of behaviour with which we are concer desirable or potentially desirable behaviour which we increase; (2) undesirable behaviour which we wish to or eliminate.

## CLASSICAL CONDITIONING

One of the pioneers of learning theory was Pavlov first person to report systematically on the relatio stimulus and response in dogs (Pavlov 1927). P ing experience, the dogs in Pavlov's experimer

behaviour which we see as the goal of treatmen
ficient for us to help a child to be able to adjust h
a way which he can achieve within the comparati
residential community. He must also be able to
learnt acceptable behaviour to situations outsid
such as home and school.

The two major approaches to treatment whic
from learning theory are (1) behaviour modifica
the work of psychologists, led by Skinner, and e
niques of operant conditioning, often throug
token economy; (2) behaviour therapy, derived
the work of psychologists, Wolpe and Lazarus,
techniques of systematic desensitization. In ord
relevance and potential value of such technique
group therapists, the major concepts of learning
discussed under the following headings:

Classical Conditioning
Operant Conditioning:
    Through Positive Reinforcement
    Through Negative Reinforcement and Punishm
    Through Extinction
Modelling
Counter-Conditioning and Systematic Desensitizatio

The important point to bear in mind when planning a
ment strategy which aims primarily at changing behavi
precursor to a change in attitude or feeling is that there a
two major types of behaviour with which we are concer
desirable or potentially desirable behaviour which we
increase; (2) undesirable behaviour which we wish to d
or eliminate.

## CLASSICAL CONDITIONING

One of the pioneers of learning theory was Pavlov, who v
first person to report systematically on the relationship b
stimulus and response in dogs (Pavlov 1927). Before the
ing experience, the dogs in Pavlov's experiments would s

given to them but not when a bell was rung. To
ning experience a bell was rung immediately
s given on a number of occasions. After this, the
without any presentation of food was enough to
ion. Learning through this type of experience is
gh responses being evoked by new stimuli.

and experiments with human subjects proved
ally possible to condition some human responses
method. In a somewhat heartless experiment
yner (1920) established a fear of white rats in a
ert, who originally had no fear of the rats and
with them. He was, however, afraid of loud
eriments sounded a loud gong on several occa-
ert was playing with a rat, after which Albert
ved signs of fear when the rat was presented to
ugh the gong was not sounded.

given to the two types of stimuli and the two types
were: (a) 'unconditioned stimulus' and 'uncon-
onse'; and (b) 'conditioned stimulus' and 'con-
onse'. The 'unconditioned stimulus' was, in the
ov's dogs, the presentation of food followed by the
ned response', salivation; the 'conditioned
s the bell followed by the 'conditioned response' of

xtent to which a new and neutral stimulus, e.g. the bell,
conditioned to evoke a response is governed by the
of the presentation in relation to the unconditioned
s, i.e. the food. It was found that the new stimulus must
nted before the unconditioned stimulus, the food, was
d for response to the new stimulus to be established.

a residential community, therefore, we wish to elicit
w piece of desirable behaviour through the use of clas-
nditioning techniques, it is essential to present the new
stimulus just before the existing unconditioned
is. For example, meal times in a residential community
e preceded by noisy and disruptive behaviour which
when the food is actually put in front of the children and
begins. If a member of staff wishes to produce an

# 4 The Behaviourist Approach

INTRODUCTION

There are similarities between the behaviourist approach to therapy and the approach of the Transactional Analysts in that each believes in the possibility of change and each employs techniques which concentrate on working with the positive, or potentially positive, aspects of a personality. The major difference between the two theoretical standpoints is that, whereas the T.A. therapist is helping the child through his own awareness of the negative influences of his previous experience and an insight into his attitudes and emotional responses, the behaviourist is primarily interested in present observable behaviour and does not think it important to trace the antecedents of this behaviour or to gain insight into thoughts and feelings for changes in behaviour to take place. Behaviour therapists base their methods on principles derived from learning theory.

Learning, in the behaviourist sense of the word, can be defined as a relatively permanent change in behaviour which occurs as a result of prior experience, although the change may not be apparent until a situation arises in which the new learning can be demonstrated. Learning, therefore, is a change in behaviour *potential* and is one way of describing what we are hoping to achieve with the children who live in our residential communities. Many of them come to us with an unhelpful and self-destructive set of learnt behaviours, such as going into each new experience aggressively or even violently or, at the other extreme, tending to withdraw into an inner world or shell when under some real or imagined threat. Whatever therapeutic intervention we employ, no matter what the theoretical basis for our methods, it is this potential for relatively permanent change in

*Figure 3(6a)* Joining dots − problem

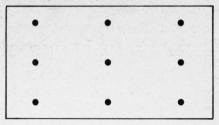

*Figure 3(6b)* Joining dots − solution

Start here

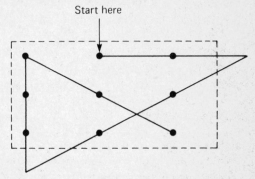

himself, draw up, in writing, individual contracts within the following frame:

What do I need to do...?
What am I willing to do...?
Whom can I ask for help...?
Whom do I trust to measure my progress...?

SUMMARY

In this chapter it was assumed that the reader had understood and familiarized himself with the theories of Transactional Analysis described in the previous chapter. Each of the major principles of T.A. as a therapy was examined in the light of group exercises which would enable members of a therapy group to be helped by that principle. Above all the T.A. belief that it is possible to change one's self-image from 'not O.K.' to 'O.K.' and one's life script from a 'loser script' to a 'winner script' was stressed.

atmosphere of calm prior to the serving of the food, he could use a new conditioned stimulus such as clapping his hands loudly and waiting for silence just before the food is served. If the conditioning is successful the children will learn to be quiet when they hear the clap and peace can be established before the food is served and in other situations.

One of Pavlov's findings in relation to classical conditioning is extremely relevant to residential therapy. He discovered that if the bell, to the sound of which the dogs had been conditioned to salivate, was rung repeatedly without the presentation of any food, salivation would decrease and eventually stop. Staff must not be surprised, therefore, if, having achieved an easy method of controlling noise in the dining room, they find that when they start to allow a long delay between the clap and the food being served, children return to their previous pattern of noisy chaos before a meal. This kind of return to the previous type of behaviour, which the staff thought they had successfully extinguished, is termed 'spontaneous recovery' and can dishearten staff who thought that the undesirable behaviour had disappeared for ever. It has been found, however, that 'booster' injections of the previous conditioning process produce a relatively rapid return to the desired behaviour in response to the conditioned stimulus.

Pavlov, extending his experiments on the relationship between a particular conditioned stimulus and a response, discovered that, once a response had been conditioned to a particular stimulus, it was unnecessary to present that exact stimulus for the response to occur. Slight variations of the stimulus would also produce the response. This process he termed 'generalization' and, in the case of Albert and the rat, it could be seen to be in operation in that Albert began to react fearfully not only to the rat but also to anything furry such as a rabbit or a fur coat.

Many of the children who come into our residential communities demonstrate this generalized response to certain stimuli, e.g. if an adult reaches out to touch them their reflex action is to flinch in anticipation of a blow as opposed to a caress. A teacher, parent, or houseparent who has previously produced a reflex response of fear and mistrust in a child may have caused, through this process of generalization, the child to fear all adults he meets who stand in one of these relationships to him. Similarly, if the residential therapist is successful in producing a new set of trusting and caring responses in a child, the child may start to respond to other adults in authority roles with a similar trust and warmth.

Classical conditioning is perhaps not one of the most useful techniques of behavioural treatment, as it is most effective in conditioning reflex responses mediated by the autonomic nervous system such as salivation or heart rate. It does have its uses, however, and certainly an understanding of this first principle of learning theory is of value to the staff in a residential community.

OPERANT CONDITIONING – THROUGH POSITIVE
REINFORCEMENT

Operant conditioning differs from classical conditioning in three major respects:

(1) In classical conditioning the unconditioned stimulus, i.e. the food for Pavlov's dogs, is given irrespective of the dog's behaviour. In operant conditioning the subject's own behaviour is what decides what the unconditioned stimulus will be.
(2) In classical conditioning the time allowed to lapse between the conditioned stimulus and the unconditioned stimulus is always the same and remains rigidly fixed. In operant conditioning the time lapse depends on the subject's own behaviour.
(3) In classical conditioning the conditioned response, e.g. the salivation and the unconditioned response, are similar if not identical, whereas in operant conditioning they are usually quite different.

The fact that operant conditioning uses the subject's own behaviour in a more flexible time span to produce new responses makes this technique of influencing behaviour more practical and more versatile than classical conditioning and is the technique most widely used in behaviourist treatment.

B. F. Skinner (1938) was, and still is, one of the most important investigators into operant conditioning. His hypothesis was that it would be possible to increase and influence desired behaviours by using responses already demonstrated by the subject and following these responses with reinforcement so that the strength of the responses would be increased. To test this hypothesis Skinner devised a piece of apparatus, the 'Skinner Box', which is designed so that when a rat in the box presses, at first by chance, a metal bar, it receives a food pellet. The rat will continue to make a variety of movements but each time it presses the bar it receives a food pellet. If this response continues to be rewarded, the rat will gradually learn to press the bar every time and other types of responses will decrease.

When we observe the behaviour of children in a residential community it is clear to see that many of their most common behaviours have been learnt through this pattern of reinforcement, e.g. a child accidentally wets the bed one night and finds that he receives a great deal of attention from his mother who normally does not pay much attention to him round bed-time or in the early morning because she has three younger children. If this 'accident' occurs on several occasions and receives a similar high degree of attention, it is likely to become a regular response in the child's repertoire of attention-seeking behaviours. As has been discussed earlier, many children who are placed in residential communities have found that their most effective way of attracting attention, albeit anger or annoyance, is through anti-social behaviours such as swearing, fighting, bed-wetting, or refusing to speak.

If we are to use operant conditioning successfully to modify anti-social behaviours and encourage the development of acceptable or potentially acceptable responses in the children, we must take the following six steps:

(1) The exact behaviour which we are trying to change must be defined in terms of observable behaviour. It is not enough to state as a treatment goal that a child should be more

co-operative with staff. This general goal must be broken down into small, easily identifiable pieces of behaviour, e.g. he should obey a command immediately; he should not swear at other children or staff; he should not hit other children; he should take his turn, on a consistent and observable rota, to wash the dishes.

(2) Having defined the behaviour to be changed, it is necessary to observe, over a significant time span, e.g. a week or two, how frequently and to what degree the behaviour takes place. This is called 'obtaining a base line'. Sometimes staff who find a particular piece of behaviour from one child very irritating are apt to exaggerate the frequency of this behaviour. In order to fix treatment goals which are useful and realistic an objective rating of the actual frequency of a behaviour must be obtained before the operant conditioning process is begun.

(3) Having defined the behaviour to be modified and measured its frequency and intensity, the environment in which the operant conditioning should take place to achieve the maximum success must be carefully planned. It is no use deciding to modify Johnny's aggressive behaviour towards other children and then isolating him from all other children. Nor is it a realistic goal unless some slight potential for being friendly has been demonstrated by Johnny and can, therefore, be enhanced by reinforcement. All staff who are to be involved in the treatment must be aware of the goals in great detail, otherwise they may find themselves, by accident, reinforcing the 'wrong' behaviours.

(4) One of the most important tasks when planning a programme of behaviour modification is to determine, through observation and enquiry, what rewards are really significant to the child and so could be used as reinforcers of desirable behaviour. These will vary from child to child and may be very material, such as sweets, money, toys; or more abstract such as a smile, a privilege like staying up late or simply basking in adult or peer approval and attention. Generally speaking, the younger the child the more tangible the reward – the only danger being that, by offering a steady supply of

sweets as reinforcers to a young child, he may finish up spending a lot of his time at the dentist's surgery!

(5) Having decided on the target behaviour and the rewards to be given the first time the desirable behaviour is shown, it must be rewarded immediately and every successive time until the behaviour appears to be well established. It may be that a child whose behavioural goal, for example, is to stop fighting other children finds it very difficult to show any alternative behaviour. In a case like this the slightest piece of non-aggressive behaviour, e.g. a smile, may need to be reinforced as a preliminary goal. This process of reinforcing successive approximations of the desired behaviour is called 'shaping'.

As the treatment programme progresses, it will be necessary to introduce a variety of reinforcers and also to vary the schedule of reinforcement.

(6) As operant conditioning is a process dependent on the observation of behaviour, it is possible, and important, to record frequency and changes in the target behaviour. If there is no measurable progress, one is forced to conclude that either the goal is unrealistic or that the agents of reinforcement are not adequate and the treatment plan may have to be revised.

Each of these six steps in operant conditioning will now be discussed in more detail.

## Behaviour amenable to operant conditioning

All therapists assume an omnipotent role to some degree, even the least directive of therapists, in that, by being asked or having offered to intervene to bring about change in another person's feelings, beliefs, and/or behaviours, there is an underlying assumption that the therapist knows to some extent what these should be. Operant conditioning has proved to be a powerful and effective technique of bringing about observable changes in behaviour and therefore it is important that goals for behaviour change are set with responsibility, integrity, and a sound knowledge and experience of the underlying principles of the treatment method.

Staff in a residential community must be prepared to examine honestly their own attitudes and levels of tolerance over specific behaviours before deciding which behaviours they plan to increase or decrease through operant conditioning. Staff within the same community may have very different capacities for accepting certain behaviours such as stealing or swearing. In setting goals for behavioural change in a child, the criterion should be primarily the child's need to modify that behaviour in order to survive adequately within his own personal environment.

For example, an excellent member of staff within my own residential community happened to find swearing totally intolerable and because of this she embarked on a successful programme of behaviour modification with a girl who swore almost continuously and the majority of the swearing was eliminated. Unfortunately, in the area of Liverpool from which the girl came it was the norm to swear and when she returned home to live the fact that she no longer swore made her almost an outcast in her own environment where she was accused of 'talking posh'!

In 1928 an early study to identify which behaviours teachers found problematic was carried out in a Cleveland school by E. K. Wickman. Teachers were asked first about their attitudes to the relative seriousness of problem behaviours in the abstract and then asked to evaluate these in terms of particular children. The hierarchy of problems in *Table 4(1)* emerged.

From this study it was concluded that teachers rated as more problematic areas where children act out, e.g. stealing, than areas arising out of internalizing of problems, e.g. sensitiveness and shyness.

The order of most difficult and undesirable to the least significant behaviour problems emerged as:

(1) sex problems, stealing, dishonesty, truancy, disobedience;
(2) problems of classroom order and application to school tasks;
(3) antagonistic, aggressive personality traits;
(4) withdrawing, recessive personality traits.

TABLE 4(1) *Hierarchy of problem behaviours (Cleveland Study)*

| At the top of the league | |
| --- | --- |
| *Boys* | *Girls* |
| stealing | heterosexual activity |
| heterosexual activity | obscene talk |
| obscene talk | stealing |
| untruthfulness | smoking |
| masturbation | profanity |
| disobedience | disobedience |
| profanity | masturbation |
| impertinence (defiance) | cheating |
| cruelty and bullying | untruthfulness |
| cheating | unreliableness |
| truancy | temper tantrums |
| destructive behaviour | truancy |

| At the bottom of the league | |
| --- | --- |
| *Boys* | *Girls* |
| attracting attention | restlessness |
| tattling | tardiness |
| restlessness | nervousness |
| over critical of others | over critical of others |
| thoughtlessness | suspiciousness |
| suspiciousness | unsocialness |
| imaginative lying | physical cowardice |
| fearfulness | imaginative lying |
| unsocialness | dreaminess |
| sensitiveness | sensitiveness |
| inquisitiveness | fearfulness |
| shyness | shyness |

It is not surprising that the behaviours which caused the most concern were the more acting-out and extrovert behaviours, as these are the behaviours which most disrupt a class. In fact a child who is very withdrawn or who lives in a fantasy inner world may be much more emotionally disturbed than an aggressive child.

In order to assess the type of problem behaviours which are of concern to my own staff in our residential school for maladjusted children, I asked the teachers and child care staff how they would rank the following behaviours or personality traits as problems, based on similar categories to those used in the Cleveland study:

  aggressive personality;
  withdrawn behaviour;
  drugtaking and smoking;
  stealing;
  truancy;
  under-performing in class;
  lying;
  misbehaviour in class;
  homosexual behaviour;
  heterosexual behaviour;
  fantasizing;
  antagonizing others;
  disobedience.

The staff were asked to rank these behaviours: (1) as they presented problems to them personally as staff; (2) as they thought the children would rank them as problems to themselves, see *Table 4(2)*. It can be concluded from this simple study that the acting out behaviours still cause the most concern though, to my particular staff, withdrawn behaviour is highly ranked.

TABLE 4(2)  *Hierarchy of problem behaviours (Highfield study)*

| As problems to staff | As problems to children |
| --- | --- |
| aggressive personality | stealing |
| antagonizing others | misbehaviour in class |
| withdrawn behaviour | antagonizing others |
| drugtaking and smoking | aggressive personality |
| stealing | lying |
| truancy | withdrawn behaviour |
| lying | truancy |
| misbehaviour in class | homosexual behaviour |
| under-performing in class | under-performing in class |
| disobedience | drugtaking and smoking |
| homosexual behaviour | heterosexual behaviour |
| heterosexual behaviour | disobedience |
| fantasizing | fantasizing |

Behaviours which are selected for operant conditioning treatment are often in the category of acting-out behaviours as these are easily observable and monitored. If problems of lack of confidence and recessive personality traits can be analysed and broken down into small behavioural goals, however, (e.g. by planning to condition a very shy child to speak once an hour to one other person) then, once a day in the whole group, operant conditioning can be as effective as with the violent aggressive behaviours.

The following types of behaviours (see *Table 4(3)*) have proved, in my experience in a residential community, to be amenable to operant conditioning where other methods may have failed. I have placed them in two broad categories:

(1) acting-out behaviours; (2) withdrawn behaviours.

TABLE 4(3) *Behaviours amenable to operant conditioning*

| Acting-out behaviours | Withdrawn behaviours |
|---|---|
| (1) physical aggression − bullying, fighting, destructive behaviour and temper tantrums | (1) stammering |
| | (2) elective mutism |
| (2) verbal aggression − over-critical of others, sadistic teasing, putting others down, sarcasm | (3) fantasizing |
| | (4) fear of failure preventing the learning of new academic skills |
| (3) enuresis | (5) inability to communicate verbally |
| (4) encopresis | |
| (5) stealing | (6) over-cautiousness |
| (6) hyperactivity | (7) lying |
| (7) school refusal (as opposed to school phobia) | |

For details of successful operant conditioning research on the above types of behaviour the reader is referred to the works of Bandura (1965), Lazarus (1960), and Wolpe and Lazarus (1966).

When observing a child's behaviour it is useful to have as a rule of thumb a check list of developmental acquisitions which are 'normal' for a certain age. This helps the therapist to choose realistic goals for a child and gives a guide to the possible positive aspects of the child's behaviour to complement the negative problem aspects more readily observed.

Havighurst (1953) suggested that the following developmental tasks are the most relevant and that they can be assessed in terms of observable behaviour.

'0–6 YEARS
*Learning:*
   (1) to walk;
   (2) to take solid foods;
   (3) to talk;
   (4) to control elimination of body waste;
   (5) sex differences and sex modesty;
   (6) achieving physiological stability;
   (7) to distinguish right and wrong and develop a conscience;
   (8) to relate emotionally to others;
   (9) to form simple concepts of social and physical reality;
6–12 YEARS
*Learning (or Developing):*
   (10) physical skills necessary for ordinary games;
   (11) wholesome attitudes towards oneself;
   (12) to appropriately relate to age mates;
   (13) an appropriate masculine and feminine role;
   (15) concepts for everyday living;
   (16) conscience, morality and a scale of values;
   (17) personal independence;
   (18) attitudes towards social groups and institutions.'

For the purposes of the present discussion, the following two case studies will be used to illustrate the method of operant conditioning.

*Case Study One* – Belinda, an acting-out child

Belinda, aged 12, was the eldest of four daughters born in rapid succession to a couple whose marital relationship was put under some considerable strain through (a) an interfering grandmother and (b) lack of money and suitable accommodation for a large family. Belinda was hurried out of her babyhood by the arrival of her three sisters, two of whom were twins, and began to show aggressive and destructive behaviour, which consisted of bullying her sisters by intimidating them verbally and physically if necessary; exhibiting the same behaviour to other children who were younger than she; being cruel to insects and small animals; being verbally aggressive and disobedient in relation to authority and parent figures.

*Case Study Two* — Paul, aged 8, a withdrawn nervous child, totally lacking self-confidence

Paul was the elder of two sons, the second of whom was more intelligent, more attractive and a constant source of pride to his parents. Paul was referred for treatment when he developed a stutter and his lack of any progress at school was causing his parents to worry and to pressurize him to be 'like his brother'. In a peer group Paul would isolate himself and in class his reaction to each new challenge would be 'I can't'.

Using the above case studies as models, the next steps in designing a programme of behaviour modification, i.e. operant conditioning, will be discussed.

## Forming a base line

One of the claims of behaviourist therapy is that it is a more scientific form of intervention than other therapies as it is based solely on observable behaviour and its manipulation. When selecting target goals for behaviour change through operant conditioning, it is important to express these goals in observable and rateable behaviours. Often the general behavioural change desired will have to be broken down into a chain of small behaviours in order to obtain an accurate record of their frequencies. For example, in Case Study One, the overall goal was to eliminate Belinda's aggressive attitude to family, other children, and authority and to help her to find acceptable ways of attracting the attention of which she felt cheated because of the intense competition from her sisters. This overall goal was broken down into the following set of individual goals:

(1) to speak non-aggressively to sisters and peers unless under extreme and deliberate provocation;

(2)  to refrain from hitting another child;
(3)  to refrain from 'answering back' to authority figures;
(4)  to refrain from hurting insects;
(5)  to increase her latent, though observable, capacity for helping another child.

Having defined the exact behavioural goals, the next step is to measure the frequency and duration of each of the responses involved in the programme in order to be accurate about the intensity of the problem and in order to monitor changes in the behaviours. This procedure is called 'forming a base line'.

Ideally, the observer who is forming the base line should be able to detach himself from interaction with the subject child and should rate the behaviours over a significant time span.

The simplest way of recording the frequency of a behaviour under observation is to use a small pocket calculator which can be held unobtrusively and which can add one to the total each time the behaviour is observed. If more than one behaviour at a time is under observation, the behaviours can be labelled A, B, or C and the record of frequency can be kept by placing a mark on a sheet of paper each time the particular behaviour occurs.

*Behaviour A* — Speaking in an aggressive tone of voice.

For a different two hours each day for a week observe the child and for each time she speaks in an unduly aggressive tone of voice put a mark against the behaviour.

*Behaviour B* — Hitting another child.

Repeat rating as for Behaviour A.

*Behaviour C* — Answering back to authority figures.

Repeat as for A and B.

The base line from this observation could be like the record in *Figure 4(1)*. The most frequent response may be chosen as the first target behaviour to be modified or the therapist may choose to start with the least frequent behaviour.

The therapist may decide to concentrate on forming a base line from observation of a specific behaviour at the same time

*Figure 4(1)* Example of a recorded base line

*Day one*
8.00 a.m. to 10.00 a.m.
    A      / / / / / /
    B      / /
    C      / / / / / / / / /

*Day two*
10.00 a.m. to 12.00 noon
    A      / / / /
    B      / / /
    C      / / / / /

*Day three*
12.00 noon to 2.00 p.m.
    A      / / / / / / / / / /
    B      / / /
    C      / / /

*Day four*
2.00 p.m. to 4.00 p.m.
    A      / / / / / /
    B      /
    C      / / /

*Day five*
4.00 p.m. to 6.00 p.m.
    A      / / / /
    B      / / /
    C      / / / /

*Day six*
6.00 p.m. to 8.00 p.m.
    A      / / / / / / /
    B      / /
    C      / / / /

*Day seven*
8.00 p.m. to 10.00 p.m.
    A      / / /
    B      /
    C

*Totals for the week:*
    Behaviour A — speaking aggressively    41
    Behaviour B — hitting another child    15
    Behaviour C — answering back    28

*Figure 4(2)* Base line data taken between the same times each day

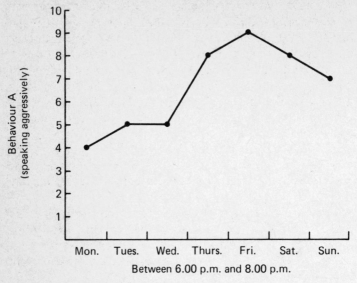

Between 6.00 p.m. and 8.00 p.m.

each day because this appears to be the most problematic time of the day for the child under observation. Ratings could then be shown on a graph as in *Figure 4(2)*.

If the duration of a particular behaviour is significant, this can be timed by an observer with a watch or stop watch who records the length of time the child spends on that behaviour each time it occurs.

For example, if we look at Case Study Two, we might have broken down the overall goal of helping Paul to become more self-confident and less isolated from his peers into the following steps:

(A) to spend time playing with another child instead of alone;
(B) to speak to one adult once an hour;
(C) to say, 'I can' instead of 'I can't' once in every school lesson.

It is important to know just how much time Paul is spending alone and to determine this the observer must record not only each time Paul chooses to isolate himself but also for what length of time.

Another significant variable when establishing a base line before designing a programme of behaviour modification through operant conditioning is to note, once the frequency and duration of the problem behaviour under observation has been determined, in which situations or in the presence of which other peers or adults the behaviour occurs most noticeably. It is not uncommon for staff in a residential community to find that a particular child may be leading a Jekyll and Hyde existence in that his behaviour is totally different within the community from the behaviour described at home and school. Some person or factor in the environment is responsible for producing and reinforcing a problematic behavioural response and the therapist must take this into consideration when planning the programme.

Having selected the behaviour or behaviours to be modified and obtained an accurate record of their occurrence to form a base line, the next step for the therapist is to ensure that there is an environment and a setting which will be conducive to operant conditioning.

## Ensuring the appropriate environment

In many ways a residential community is an ideal situation in which to attempt operant conditioning as many of the facets of a child's daily life are under the observation and control of staff. Although behaviourists place more importance on behaviour itself than on understanding the attitudes or feelings which accompany the behaviour, they do not discount the importance of feelings or the necessity for the successful behaviour therapist to establish a trusting relationship with the child with whom he is working. This will in fact be an essential in the programme of behaviour modification as approval or lack of approval from the therapist will form one of the most powerful reinforcers of desired behaviour. As the resident therapist is living closely with the child, he is in a good position to win his trust and affection before involving him in the plan to change some of his behaviour.

It is important also that other members of staff not directly involved in the treatment understand and co-operate with the aims of the therapist, otherwise they may inadvertently be working against the programme and failing to reinforce the desired behaviours. They may even reinforce unwittingly the behaviour to be changed. For example, the therapist may be planning to modify a child's habit of speaking aggressively to other children by ignoring him when he speaks in this way and rewarding him tangibly or with praise when he speaks in a non-aggressive tone. If another member of staff continues to berate the child when he speaks aggressively and ignore him when he makes the effort to speak politely, he will be undoing all of the therapist's hard work.

Other essentials in the therapeutic environment for this type of therapy are those which are important for any therapy within a residential community. There should be an atmosphere of safety and security from threats from without the community, e.g. fear of unexpected removal from that community, and from threats from within the community, e.g. intolerable teasing or bullying by peers or staff. Consistency of staff atttitude and behaviour both in the caring and controlling of the children is also important. Other factors in the environment, such as the provision of suitable models on which children can base their behaviour, will be discussed later.

**Positive reinforcement**

'A reinforcer is any stimulus which strengthens the frequency, speed, or magnitude of a response.' (Jehu 1967:27) A reinforcer is different from a reward, as rewards do not always have the effect of strengthening desired behaviour. Some children in a residential community will have been rewarded or bribed to be 'good' with expensive gifts or privileges and yet this seems to have had no effect on their 'bad' behaviour. Other children will have found that the reward of attention from adults can only be achieved through anti-social behaviour. The secret of successful use of positive reinforcement in promoting desirable behaviour is to find the appropriate *addition* of something to a child's situation which will increase his response as opposed to the *removal* of something from a child's situation involved in negative reinforcement (see p. 112).

There are two types of positive reinforcers: primary and secondary. Primary reinforcers are stimuli related to our basic biological needs, e.g. food, water, sexual contact. When one observes how these basic needs are met from infancy onwards, it can be seen that the meeting of these needs is often accompanied by the giving of attention, approval, or affection. Thus any stimulus which is frequently paired with a primary reinforcer, e.g. affection with the giving of food or sexual comfort, becomes in itself an agent of reinforcement and is called a secondary reinforcer. Some secondary reinforcers which have been paired with more than one primary reinforcer become generalized reinforcers in that they can be seen to reinforce more than one type of behaviour. The most common of these generalized reinforcers are money, attention, and affection.

As a child develops he will also gradually learn to rely on self-reinforcement to maintain some of his behaviours. Approved behaviour may be reinforced from within by thoughts such as 'I did well to finish all my homework' or 'I did well not to lose my temper when Jane annoyed me'. Such thoughts have acquired reinforcement potential through their association with primary or other secondary reinforcers such as a good mark for homework or praise for keeping one's temper.

When a therapist is choosing which positive reinforcers to use to encourage the development of a desired behaviour, it is important to look at the child's personal history to ascertain which types of reinforcers seem to have promoted which behaviours.

Many children in a residential community have been starved of unconditional affection and may have learnt to demand a show of physical affection from all adults indiscriminately as a prerequisite to performing any socially acceptable behaviour. We are all familiar with the child living in a residential community who is 'all over' any stranger who sets foot over the threshold! Unfortunately, this desperate need for affection and attention may have led a child to escalate undesirable behaviours which, in his experience, have at least produced attention.

It may be advisable when planning a programme for this type of child to use a less loaded secondary reinforcer than attention. One might use a tangible reward such as a sweet, given with a fairly neutral attitude, to reinforce a desired piece of behaviour, e.g. sitting for ten minutes, while watching television, without interrupting.

One of the advantages of attempting operant conditioning within a residential community is that, as much of the child's life takes place within that community, there is a good variety of positive reinforcers or 'rewards' to choose from and to tailor to a specific child's needs. Time spent with a favourite adult, privileges such as staying up late or choosing which television programme to watch, going out on a special expedition, being allowed to help in some interesting project, having time alone; all may be used as well as the usual tangible rewards such as pocket money, sweets, toys, books, or tokens which can be saved and traded in later for a chosen reward. There are many potential positive reinforcers which can be given to the child when he performs the desired behaviour which we are trying to increase and selecting the most effective for each child will rely on the observational skills of the therapist.

### Operant conditioning – through negative reinforcement and punishment

The other form of reinforcement employed in operant conditioning is negative reinforcement. Many pieces of behaviour which help us to avoid negative consequences are contained in our repertoire of behaviours and these are maintained through negative reinforcement. In positive reinforcement a response is strengthened by the addition of a reward; in negative reinforcement a response is strengthened by the removal of something from the situation.

Negative reinforcement is often confused with punishment. Whereas punishment is usually used to weaken a response, negative reinforcement is used to strengthen a response. The removal or withdrawal of any unpleasant stimulus after a response is made acts as a negative reinforcer. For example, a housemother who stops shouting at a child once he has done as he was told or who gives into a child in order to stop temper tantrums is negatively reinforcing that behaviour. If a child has been sent to his room for having misbehaved and he begins to cry, a member of staff may say, 'You can come out of your room when you stop crying!' If he is allowed to come out the minute he stops crying the response 'not to cry' has been strengthened because the aversive condition of being made to stay in the room has been removed. Negative reinforcement of 'not crying' has been employed. Punishment, on the other hand, is the use of an aversive stimulus, e.g. spanking, withdrawal of privileges, to reduce a response.

In Skinner's experiments with rats, when the rat pressed a lever to remove an electric shock, lever pressing was negatively reinforced and the behaviour was strengthened; when pressing the lever a shock was administered, lever pressing was punished and began to occur less frequently.

Another common form of punishment is the removal of positive reinforcers. When a child who usually earns his pocket money for good behaviour has his pocket money taken away for bad behaviour, he is being punished. The removal of the positive reinforcer of adult approval can be a powerful means of punishing a child who values that adult's approval.

Punishment, as opposed to the use of negative reinforcement, is not used in operant conditioning, or as rarely as possible, because it has proved less effective than reinforcement. Although punishment may have a temporary effect on bad behaviour, the behaviour is likely to re-occur when the punishment stops or may produce other equally undesirable behaviours. For example, a child who is severely punished for misbehaviour in the residential community may run away. Alternatively, he may become suspicious of or aggressive to the adult who punishes him or covered in exaggerated shame and guilt, which causes him to opt out of interaction with that adult.

Although punishment rarely reinforces desired behaviour, it can reinforce the desire to punish in the member of staff who has his behaviour temporarily reinforced in that punishment can appear to produce instant control. The member of staff who uses punishment as a constant technique of control is likely

TABLE 4(4) *Differences between positive reinforcement, negative reinforcement, and punishment*

| Desired behaviour | Verbal approach | Method of reinforcement | Type of reinforcement |
|---|---|---|---|
| Helping to wash the dishes | Wash up and I'll give you a sweet | Reward presented | Positive |
| Helping to wash the dishes | If you don't wash up I'll take your pocket money away from you | Reward withdrawn | Punishment |
| Helping to wash the dishes | Wash up and you can go out to play | Aversive condition (staying in) terminated | Negative |

to find that, for some children, the scale of the punishment has to escalate to have any effect whatsoever and no real change in behaviour is taking place.

To illustrate the differences between positive reinforcement, punishment, and negative reinforcement, *Table 4(4)* may be of value.

## Operant conditioning – through extinction

Changes in behaviour through operant conditioning are most often brought about through the use of positive reinforcement of desirable behaviour and sometimes through the use of negative reinforcement. It is possible also to weaken undesirable behaviour by ignoring it, i.e. not rewarding it with attention and in behaviourist terms this is called 'extinction'.

The use of extinction in operant conditioning was demonstrated by Harris, Wolf, and Baer (1964) who set out to diminish excessive crying over mild frustrations in a four-year-old boy. From systematic observation of the boy at school in the morning a base line of, on average, eight crying episodes a morning was recorded. These episodes consistently attracted the attention and concern of the teacher who, in the experiment, was asked to ignore the behaviour for ten days and only give him attention for self-help behaviour. During the last five days the crying was observed only once.

To test whether positive reinforcement of attention had previously strengthened the behaviour, the teacher was asked to give him attention again if he cried. This she did and the crying behaviour rapidly reached its former frequency. When the crying was again ignored, however, the behaviour rapidly disappeared again.

The easiest behaviour to extinguish by this method of ignoring it when it occurs is behaviour which has previously been maintained by continuous positive reinforcement. When choosing which behaviours to modify by ignoring them, it is important to ascertain that this is a behaviour which was heavily reinforced through rewards and to know the exact nature of the rewards which were used as positive reinforcers.

One of the most common forms of positive reinforcement to be seen in a residential community is the giving of attention to undesirable behaviour. This will probably also have happened to the child before he entered the community. Unfortunately, it is often easier said than done to ignore bad behaviour because that behaviour may be harmful to other members of the community. It is impossible to ignore totally a child who is physically attacking another child and difficult to ignore the behaviour of a child who is physically abusing himself, e.g. the suicidal or anorexic child. Behaviours in this category respond better to a treatment programme which combines the use of positive reinforcement for alternative and incompatible behaviour with ignoring the undesired behaviour. For example, if a child has been rewarded with attention every time he wets the bed a combination of ignoring him each time the bed is wet but rewarding him heavily when it is dry is likely to be effective.

Other behaviours which have proved difficult to modify through extinction alone are those which have been formerly maintained through the use of negative reinforcement. Once a child has learnt a response to avoid a painful aversive stimulus, e.g. throwing a temper tantrum and refusing to sit still at the dentist's surgery, this will result in him avoiding potentially painful treatment. The avoidance behaviour is strongly maintained by fear and the use of extinction, ignoring the response, is unlikely to be effective.

One of the most discouraging aspects of the use of extinction is that, initially, a behaviour which has been heavily rewarded and is then totally ignored is likely to increase in the child's desperate attempt to gain his habitual positive reinforcement. The old saying that something may have to get worse before it gets better is particularly applicable to behaviour which is being changed through extinction. It is important, therefore, that if a treatment plan for a child in a residential community includes ignoring a particular piece of undesirable behaviour, all staff should be meticulous in carrying this out and should not become discouraged when the behaviour initially becomes more pronounced.

## Schedules of reinforcement

Having decided on the behaviour changes to be treated through operant conditioning and identified the agents of reinforcement to be used, the next step is to plan the programme of reinforcement. There are two different ways in which positive reinforcement can be given (1) by ratio schedules and (2) by interval schedules.

When a ratio schedule is used the therapist gives a reward after the child has given a number of the desired responses, e.g. a child may be given a reward after he has not wet the bed for a certain number of nights. If the ratio is fixed, e.g. that the reward is given for every two nights that the child is dry, response is usually high as long as the number of non-reinforced responses is sufficiently low and the child does not have to wait a long time for his good behaviour to be reinforced. It is better, therefore, to use a small reward more frequently, e.g. a packet of sweets for every two nights that the child's bed is dry, than to promise him a bicycle if he does not wet the bed for a month. Not surprisingly the desired behaviour falls off slightly after the reward has been given and then increases in anticipation of the next predictable reward time. It has been found, however, that, when employing a fixed ratio schedule, it is possible to increase the ratio slowly, e.g. rewarding every two nights, then every four nights, then every eight nights, until the ratio is very high (Skinner 1953).

Reinforcement can also be given on a less predictable schedule and this is then termed variable-ratio reinforcement. Variable-ratio schedules are characterized by a steady rate of responding but no great dramatic change in behaviour. The hypothesis when using this type of schedule is that the child, because he does not know exactly when to expect the reward, will try hard all the time to produce the desired behaviour in the hope that each time may be the reward time. Skinner found that rats would press a lever and pigeons would peck at a very fast rate on a variable-ratio schedule in hopes of the reward of food and humans who enjoy gambling are prepared to repeat a piece of behaviour in the hope that every now and again it will be rewarded. Lundin (1961) established that the use of variable-ratio reinforcement had a long-term effect, for when the desirable behaviour was no longer maintained by the deliberate use of reinforcement this extinction process was not effective and the subject continued to behave in the desired way.

When an interval schedule of reinforcement is used, the length of time in between the reinforcement rewarding is the significant factor. When a fixed-interval schedule is used, e.g. a child will be rewarded with an apple or orange every quarter of an hour in which he does not lose his temper, there is a rapid response following reinforcement, followed by a slowing down of response until the next reinforcement. If the interval between reinforcements is long, the child finds it hard to maintain desired behaviour. Fixed-interval reinforcement has proved to be more effective than continuous reinforcement (Reese 1966), as behaviour established with such a schedule seems to continue after the conscious use of reinforcement. When a houseparent reads a story regularly at bed-time as a reinforcement of good behaviour during the evening, the child's behaviour will improve noticeably towards bed-time and hopefully this will become a piece of learnt behaviour.

Variable-interval schedules, like variable-ratio schedules,

tend to motivate the child to exhibit the desired behaviour provided, once again, that the interval between rewards is not so
great that the child loses interest and hope of reward. Someone
whose hobby is fishing is prepared to wait long intervals for the
reward of catching a fish simply because he knows that sooner
or later he is bound to catch something if he maintains his fishing. Behaviour maintained on a variable-interval schedule also
tends to continue when planned reinforcement has ceased and is
perhaps the most practical type of schedule to use if one is
working with a few children at the same time. Ratio schedules
involve keeping a record of each time each of the children in the
group performs a desired behaviour or refrains from performing an undesirable behaviour. Interval schedules are concerned
with modules of time which is an easier variable for the
therapist to manipulate.

### Recording progress and assessing results

Clearly the most important question asked concerning the use
of operant conditioning is whether the effects will last long after
the therapeutic intervention has ceased. I always quote my
husband as an example of failed behaviour modification for,
when he did National Service in the Army, he learnt to become
tidy and maintained that behaviour for two years. The minute
he was no longer under the threat of losing leave or privileges he
became his endearing untidy self again! This could well support
the opinion of Skinner, who maintains that the most effective
form of operant conditioning is through positive rather than
negative reinforcement — in my husband's case, the withdrawal
of the threat of losing leave.

The immediate effects of the conditioning programme will be
assessed by referral to the original base line. Charts and graphs
similar to those used in creating the base line can be used
to record the strengthening of desirable behaviours and the
weakening of undesirable behaviours.

The acid test of the treatment, however, will be whether the
desired behaviour persists after the programme of behaviour
modification has ceased. As we have seen when discussing

extinction and schedules of reinforcement there is often a regression to former behaviour immediately after the reinforcement has ceased but, if the conditioning has been successful, it will disappear spontaneously within time or with occasional 'booster' injections of positive reinforcement.

In my own residential community I have observed behaviour which was thought to have been successfully extinguished somewhat disconcertingly reappear when a child is under stress or is feeling insecure. This often happens in the few weeks prior to a child leaving our residential special school to return home and into mainstream education. We have found from experience, however, that this is usually a temporary regression and that, once the hurdle has been jumped, the undesirable behaviour disappears again quite rapidly.

In order to ensure that the operant conditioning has been successful, it is vital to observe the child over a significant length of time after conditioning has ceased and to give him the opportunity to live in a situation which is not specifically geared to maintaining his desirable behaviour. This gives the therapist and child alike time to discover whether the behaviour has been adequately learnt and to reintroduce short additional periods of operant conditioning should this seem necessary.

The therapist himself, who will have formulated the original base line, will bear the brunt of recording progress but he may wish to enlist the help of colleagues or, where a peer group is heavily involved in the behaviour change, other children. Many parents are also prepared to continue the behaviour modification when their child is at home for week-ends or holidays and if the method is explained carefully to them and they are shown how to record accurately, there is no reason why they should not take part and indeed, through this approval or withdrawal of approval or with tangible rewards, become one of the agents of reinforcement. As it is in the home and not in the residential community that the child must be able to survive happily, feedback from home about a child's progress is most important and should be built into the observation, recording, and assessment programme.

The secret in treating children successfully through operant conditioning lies in selecting behaviours which the therapist, through adequate knowledge of the child's developmental and social history and detailed observation of the child's behaviour in varied settings, feels have been 'learnt' responses in the first place. The danger is that, in the desire to be 'scientific' and to ignore any aspect of a child's personality which cannot be observed and measured behaviourally, the behaviours selected for treatment through operant conditioning may be trivial and of no real problem to the child or society anyway.

The other temptation is to select only those behaviours which are 'acting out' or extrovert such as being disobedient, aggressive, or destructive and to ignore the potential of the method to enhance self-esteem, confidence, and an ability to come out of one's shell. Staff in a residential community may be tempted to use operant conditioning solely as a means to gain control of difficult children and indeed teaching a child to control his own anti-social behaviour is very important but I would suggest that behaviour modification has much wider uses and that positive reinforcement used to enhance a child's 'good' behaviour can be as rewarding for therapist and child as the extinguishing of 'bad behaviour'.

## MODELLING

All cultures use models to transmit their concept of desirable behaviour patterns and value systems to the rising generation and to teach children some of the skills necessary for survival in that community. National heroes such as Winston Churchill and Davy Crockett and religious figures such as Jesus Christ and the prophet, Mohammed, are held up as worthy examples of a human being on whom to model oneself and, nowadays, television heroes as well as the great heroes of literature have joined the throng. Children imitate adult behaviour when they play with toys which are replicas of adult equipment, e.g. cots and prams, cars and tricycles, washing machines and tool sets, and the role play in games like 'house', 'doctors and nurses', 'school', 'cops and robbers', is based on observation of adult models.

Modelling in behaviourist terms is defined as the tendency to reproduce the behaviour of living or symbolic models. Miller and Dollard (1941) maintained that modelling tended to occur when an adequately motivated observer was positively reinforced for making the appropriate responses of a model in a situation which was initially trial and error. For example, a junior member of staff searching for methods by which to gain control of a difficult child may observe her senior colleagues in similar situations. The junior may try several of the observed methods, e.g. spanking, sending the child to his room, ignoring him, in a trial and error procedure. The junior member of staff will tend to model future controlling behaviour on that of the senior member of staff whose method was most effective and was rewarded with success and praise from superiors.

There is some discussion among learning theorists as to whether or not reinforcement is an important condition for the acquisition of modelled responses. What does emerge clearly is that reinforcement is necessary for the continued performance of a piece of new behaviour acquired through modelling.

As a residential community is a microcosm of society with a distinct culture of its own providing a variety of adults and peers on whom a child may model, it is important for the members of staff to be responsibly aware of the models of behaviour that exist within their community. Planned exploitation and manipulation of the principles of modelling can be a powerful tool in the hands of a residential therapist.

Three of the major observable effects of modelling are: (1) the acquisition of new responses and skills; (2) previously acquired responses may be inhibited or disinhibited depending on the behaviour displayed by the model and the consequences of that behaviour for the model; (3) a latent or somewhat neutral response in the repertoire of the child's behaviour may be triggered off by observation of the model. We shall look at these three aspects of modelling in more detail.

## The acquisition of new responses and skills

As a child develops many of his life skills are learnt through copying or modelling on adults and other children who are close to him in his daily life. In learning to overcome physical danger, the child cannot be left to experiment with different responses until he achieves the right one which can then be reinforced, for, if he makes too many wrong trial and error responses, he may not live to reach the right one! Parents and older siblings, therefore, model appropriate safety behaviours when they show a child how to cross the road or how to boil a pan of water safely. Many new motor skills are transmitted through modelling, e.g. walking and playing cricket, and human models are supplemented by symbolic models such as instructions or diagrams showing how to assemble a toy or piece of equipment.

Staff in a residential community will spontaneously teach children new physical skills through modelling, e.g. tying shoe laces, fastening buttons, and using the play and work equipment within the establishment. The important factor to keep in mind when selecting the new skills to be taught is the developmental stage of the child. One should match the teaching of new skills to the appropriate maturational stage of the child. It is useless, for example, to initiate toilet training until a child has the physical ability to control his sphincter muscles. If staff do attempt to teach a child to run before he can walk in the learning of any new physical skill they are bound to meet with frustration which is likely to be interpreted by the child as disapproval and may bring about a fear response in relation to the learning of that skill.

The residential therapist will also be concerned with teaching children social skills and here again modelling is a powerful means of transmitting desirable behaviours. A child usually learns to dress himself, to eat properly, and to develop self-care skills through copying adults but more subtle social skills, such as appropriate sex role behaviours, will also be learnt through modelling.

It is important in a residential community, therefore, that the staff group contains members of both sexes who are confident in their own sex role and provide acceptable models of a man and a woman, a husband and a wife, a father and a mother. If children are to grow up with the capacity for making happy heterosexual relationships they will need successful models not only of their own sex but also of the opposite sex. Ideally, therefore, a residential community would always employ both men and women and individuals who are secure and happy in their own sex role. To reiterate a point already made, the ability of staff to form satisfactory relationships within their own group will be one of the most powerful means of transmitting a desirable value system, through modelling, to the children.

The enhancing of verbal skills in children is also an important aspect of the behaviour therapist's role, as a child who cannot communicate adequately through putting his thoughts into words is likely to become more and more isolated and withdrawn. Autistic and elective or selective mute children are the most worrying of children with talking difficulties. The use of modelling combined with reinforcement has proved effective in helping such children to communicate and the research of psychologists in this field has produced interesting results. Lovaas (1966) filmed an experiment with a girl who would not talk in which he employed a combination of modelling and reinforcement to teach the girl to speak. To ensure that modelling could take place, he sat directly in front of the girl and physically persuaded her to maintain eye contact with him throughout the experiment. He asked the girl to name the colour of a yellow crayon which he held in front of her. At first she responded with bizarre arm movements and facial expressions. He began to slap the girl and then used negative reinforcement by refraining from slapping her when she said the word 'yellow'. As a further means to augmenting the child's attentiveness to modelling cues, food and expressions of affection were used as positive reinforcers. In this type of treatment for verbal difficulties, the therapist displays or models progressively more complex forms of verbal behaviour and rewards increasingly closer reproductions of the modelled responses. The treatment of stuttering and other speech difficulties can also be effective through the use of a combination of modelling and positive reinforcement techniques.

Many children in a residential community have been language deprived or come from families where language has been used destructively to hurt another person. In a therapeutic community, therefore, it is important for children to be surrounded by models who use language to help each other and to facilitate understanding, affection, and honest communication.

The moral development of children within his care will also be of concern to the residential therapist and through his own moral code, explicit and implicit, he will be modelling moral values for the children. Bandura and MacDonald (1963) describe an experiment in which children were seen to be heavily influenced in their moral judgements through the process of modelling. Two groups of children, who were very subjective and self-centred in their moral judgements, were formed. The experimental group was allowed to observe and listen to a group of adult models expressing objective and non-self-centred moral judgements. The control group had no exposure to the models but the children were positively reinforced whenever they expressed objective moral judgements that were unlike their usual self-centred judgements. In assessing post-experimental attitudes, the group for whom models had been provided was found to have been much more influenced to produce objective moral judgements than the group where positive reinforcement alone had been used. For staff to say, 'Do as I say, not as I do,' therefore, the impact of their advice is likely to have much less force than when staff are prepared to do themselves what they are advising the children to do.

A child's repertoire of emotional responses will also be influenced by the range of emotions modelled for him by staff and peers. Staff are sometimes recommended, in a residential community, not to show their feelings. If we are to model successful ways of coping with the wide range of emotional responses, from anger to love, which combine to produce an emotionally well-balanced person, we are doing the children a disservice if we pretend that we ourselves are without conflicting emotions. To witness staff coping successfully with potentially destructive or self-destructive emotions such as anger, grief, and fear is as important as witnessing staff delight in the emotions of joy and love. Children can and will enter vicariously into the emotional experiences of their close adults and this is one way in which they learn and rehearse a growing range of emotions.

### Inhibiting or disinhibiting of previously acquired responses

The provision of modelled behaviour for a child to imitate can be used to inhibit or disinhibit responses which the child already possesses. One factor which influences whether or not a child will imitate a model's behaviour is the observable consequences of that behaviour for the model. Sometimes these consequences are rewarding, e.g. a child who helps his housemother to tidy the room is allowed to stay up late and is rewarded with high status in his group, or punishing, e.g. a child who deliberately destroys a toy is sent to bed early and loses status in his group. Chittenden (1942) in an early experiment to show the effects of modelling formed a group of children who were excessively domineering and hyperaggressive. He showed the group a series of eleven 15-minute plays in each of which dolls, representing young children, acted out either an aggressive solution or a co-operative solution to interpersonal conflicts in the type of circumstances with which the children watching were familiar. The consequences for the models who chose aggressive solutions were shown to be unpleasant and the consequences for the models who chose co-operative solutions were shown to be rewarding. Under observation in games played in pairs after the experiment, the children who had seen the plays showed a marked improvement in their capacity to play co-operatively, while children from a control group who had not seen the film were still very aggressive in this play.

In a later attempt to inhibit the aggressive behaviour of children, Gittelman (1965) used role play with a group of very aggressive children. First he asked the children to identify and describe the type of situations which aroused aggressive responses in themselves. He then arranged these in a hierarchy from the least to the most aggression-provoking and the children role-played the situations in that order and attempted to find less aggressive solutions to the problems being enacted. Video-recording of this type of modelling treatment would enable a therapist and children to rehearse, vicariously, more desirable behaviour.

If the residential group therapist wishes to exploit the therapeutic potential of children modelling on the rewarded acceptable behaviour of other children, it is important that, when forming children into sub-groups within the community, a variety of potential models is provided. For instance, it is useful for extrovert, hyperactive children to live closely to more introvert and withdrawn children so that each may observe and copy the acceptable behaviours of his opposite personality type.

Modelling can be equally effective in disinhibiting certain behaviours. In one, now famous, experiment (Walters and Llewellyn, 1963) a group of adults who would not normally dream of inflicting pain on fellow human beings, was asked to assist in an experiment to study the effects of punishment on learning. They were given some sample shocks to make sure that they were aware of their painful nature and then required to administer shocks to the members of the experimental group whenever they responded incorrectly to a set task. (The experimental group members were, of course, confederates of the experimenter and the shocks were simulated, although this was unknown to those administering 'the shock'.) Next the subjects were shown an extremely violent film, *Rebel Without a Cause*, in which very violent flick knife fights took place. The strength of the shocks administered after seeing the film increased.

One of the questions raised by these types of experimental results is whether we should allow children to watch violent films, plays, or documentaries on television or at the theatre and cinema. Most residential communities operate some form of censorship over what children are allowed to watch but it is sometimes true to say that there are more taboos about showing children sexual activity than about showing them violence and that psycho-analytically biased staff would maintain that the vicarious participation in violence through observing it on a screen is cathartic and of benefit to the latently aggressive child. Behaviourists would not agree.

The more constructive use of modelling techniques to

disinhibit previously learnt responses is in the treatment of fears and avoidance responses.

In treating extremely withdrawn children who were fearful of other children, O'Connor (1969) showed a group of such children a series of films in which children who were themselves withdrawn and isolated from their peers were encouraged, through positive reinforcement, to join in games and interaction with their peers increasingly as the experiment progressed. The experimental group showed a marked increase in social interaction after watching these films where they had been able to observe the happy, positive consequences for the models who increased their interaction with others on film.

In a residential community there is likely to be a percentage of children who are afraid of adults and/or peers and are fearful of any new experience. If these children are given the opportunity to observe the rewarding consequences to other more adventurous peers of their capacity to make new relationships and to meet new challenges, intellectual and physical, there is a chance that they will model their own behaviour on these less fearful children. It is important for staff to reward heavily even the tiniest new courageous response in children with these problems of extreme shyness and timidity.

### The increase of latent responses

One of the areas in which behaviour therapists believe that learning theory can have a useful application is in helping children to discover and develop their inherent or latent desirable behavioural responses. Observation and imitation of models can be one of the means through which this occurs. Children have latent undesirable as well as desirable behavioural responses and staff will often draw unwittingly on modelling theory when they choose to separate from his group a child whom they feel is, for example, potentially delinquent, in the belief that he will be destructively influenced by delinquent peers. Similarly, the concept of one 'rotten apple' child in the barrel causing all the others to become 'rotten' is firmly based on modelling theory. Staff may find it very difficult in a residential community to form groups of children within which there are no 'bad' models and where the children with highest peer group status and, therefore, the highest 'modelling' potential are those who exhibit a high degree of desirable behaviours. To counteract this it is important to reward heavily desirable behaviour when it is modelled in the hope that this behaviour response will gain high status for the particular child in the eyes of staff and peers and that the leaders in the children's group will be those children whom staff as well as peers perceive as suitable models.

Many of our children are so lacking in self-confidence and self-esteem that they do not have the courage to develop the positive personality traits and skills for which they have the potential. Sometimes the observation of another child who demonstrates those traits or skills can trigger off in the child the desire to copy and model, thus developing his latent be-havioural responses. A little boy in my residential community called Richard was undersized for his age and suffered from feelings of inferiority in relation to his peers. His ability to make friends and to develop self-esteem was severely hampered by the aggressive manner he had developed as a defence against feeling physically inferior. At one of the school functions for parents there was a display of judo given by a group of children of all sizes and ages. Richard was fascinated by the fact that the size of the child seemed to bear no relation to skill at judo and the next day he asked us if he could join a judo club. His parents report to us that since he has become a regular and successful member of the local judo club, his self-confidence has increased enormously and he no longer relates aggressively to his peers. Many apparently passive children have a potential for leader-ship or for teaching and encouraging younger children, which may be developed in a small group environment where staff and other children model this type of behaviour.

Modelling, in all its implications and potentials for behaviour change, can be seen to be a useful means of promoting healthy behaviour modification and can, when used consciously and sensitively, enhance cognitive skills, interpersonal relation-ships, and coping behaviour generally.

## Counter-conditioning and systematic desensitization

As early as 1924, behaviour therapists were experimenting successfully in reducing fears and phobias through a method which became known as counter-conditioning. In this method the therapist establishes a response in the child which is incompatible with the fear/avoidance response to the anxiety-producing object or situation and gradually the fear is eliminated. This process is termed 'reciprocal inhibition' and there are many successful experiments to prove its efficacy.

Jones (1924) described the treatment of Peter, aged three, who was afraid of rabbits, rats, and other furry objects. Feeding was chosen as the pleasurable response incompatible with the fear of fur. Before the treatment, if Peter was given sweets with an animal in the room near him, his fear was so great that he would refuse the sweets in favour of escaping from the animal. The treatment progressed in easy stages. In the first session a caged rabbit was placed in the corner of the room and Peter was given sweets which he was able to eat. Gradually, over a number of sessions, the rabbit was released while Peter ate his sweets and was brought nearer and nearer to him until finally he could hold the rabbit on his knee.

Pleasant emotional responses, such as affection and attention, or pleasant tangible rewards, such as sweets and toys, can be paired with tasks which are gradually more and more anxiety-provoking to a particular child, in order to help him overcome his specific fear or phobia. For example, some children come into a residential community with a marked fear of physical contact, especially with adults. If the residential therapist can gradually and patiently help the child to associate touch (the response he fears) with pleasurable experiences ranging from handing him a sweet to tucking him up in bed and kissing him good-night, the fear of physical contact will gradually disappear.

Many of the problems experienced by our children arouse great anxiety in the child and if we are to help them through behaviour therapy we must first help them to relax. Wolpe (1958) and Lazarus (1961) developed a method combining relaxation with counter-conditioning, which they termed 'systematic desensitization'. In the first stage of treatment the child is taught deep muscle relaxation. Methods of achieving this relaxation will be described in Chapter 5. The therapist then asks the child to list all the stimuli which arouse fear in him and these are arranged in a hierarchy from the least to the most disturbing. While in a state of relaxation, the child is then asked to imagine the least disturbing situation and encouraged to talk about it or, if it is about a specific stimulus, e.g. spiders, to look at pictures. Gradually the real stimulus is introduced and progress through the list is made until the most anxiety-provoking stimulus can finally be faced without fear.

School phobia is one of the more common phobias from which children suffer and systematic desensitization has proved to be one of the most successful means of removing a child's anxieties about going to school. Patterson (1965) describes the treatment of a child who would not stay in school unless one of his parents was present. The child also found it difficult to play with his friends outside the house without constantly returning to the house to make sure that his mother was still there.

In the first treatment session the child was given a chocolate drop for every 30-second interval that he did not look to see if his mother was still there. The mother was then asked to leave the room and sit outside the door whilst the therapist engaged in doll play with the child. During this doll play the child was rewarded with a chocolate drop every time he commented on the fact that the doll was not afraid to be alone in situations of going to school and playing with other children. These procedures proved effective and the child returned to school.

As an alternative to pairing relaxation with systematic desensitization, it is possible to use emotive imagery to help a child, especially a very young child, to overcome his fears. Lazarus and Abramovitz (1962) treated nine children with a variety of anxieties using this method. Once again a hierarchy of anxieties from least feared to most feared situations was established. Each child was asked to imagine a sequence of fearful events and the therapist wove these into stories in which the child's favourite characters appeared. When the child's imagination and emotion had been aroused the hierarchy of anxiety-provoking situations was included in the narrative. After a twelve-month follow-up study of these children the method proved to have been successful in eliminating the fears of seven of the nine children.

A residential community is an ideal setting in which to carry out systematic densitization as time is no object. Children who are afraid, for example, of travelling, of water, of animals, can be gradually desensitized to these fears through the type of counter-conditioning described above.

One more extreme form of counter-conditioning is achieved through the pairing of a noxious or aversive stimulus with the undesirable behaviour. A child who bites his nails, for example, may have his nails painted with an unpleasant-tasting substance which comes to be associated for him with the nail-biting. If the drive to avoid the nasty taste is stronger than the drive to bite his nails, the nail-biting will cease. Aversive therapy at its extreme uses pain and discomfort as the noxious stimuli and most residential social workers would find the use of this type of therapy both unethical and inappropriate in a community which aims to be therapeutic and supportive.

The use of satiation or 'flooding' can be appropriate in some situations. One of the oldest methods of discouraging a child from smoking is to encourage him to smoke his way through a packet of cigarettes until he is sick! A similar technique explored by Ullmann and Krasner (1965) was to encourage the repeated performance of the undesirable behaviour, e.g. stammering, until the response is extinguished because anxiety is no longer associated with it and the fatigue which results from this repetition makes the response painful and aversive.

SUMMARY

In this chapter the major theoretical concepts derived from learning theory have been described and their potential for behaviour modification and behaviour therapy explored: classical conditioning, operant conditioning through positive reinforcement, negative reinforcement and punishment, extinction, modelling and counter-conditioning, and systematic desensitiz-ation. Operant conditioning through positive reinforcement and the use of modelling have been seen to contain the widest potential as techniques for achieving behavioural change in a residential community though the other techniques all have something to offer.

Although behaviourist therapy approaches treatment from a scientific standpoint which relies on observation and recording of visible behaviour, the relationship of trust and acceptance between therapist and child is seen as essential and respect for his cognitive and effective processes is not undervalued.

# 5 Behaviour Group Therapy

The therapeutic potential of the major principles of learning theory discussed in the previous chapter can be exploited very effectively in group therapy. Behaviour group therapy within a residential community can either take the form of a total way of life for the entire group of children, a daily or weekly group therapy session for the entire group of children divided into manageable small groups if the community is large, or regular group therapy sessions for one small group of children selected on the basis that the majority of their maladaptive behaviours appear to have been 'learnt' as opposed to having sprung from unconscious or conscious emotional or cognitive deficiencies.

Behaviour group therapy will be discussed in this chapter under the broad headings of (1) behaviour therapy for the residential community as a whole and (2) small group behaviour therapy. Each form of group therapy will draw on the principles of operant conditioning, modelling, relaxation, and systematic desensitization and will have many basic assumptions and therapeutic techniques in common. For instance, the starting point for each child in either situation will be that he, in fact, acknowledges the need to bring about some change in his behaviour and is prepared to work on this. Observable and rate-able behaviour changes only will be specified in the treatment goals and these goals will be realistically within the capacity of the individual, or, where a group goal is specified, the group. When desired changes in behaviour are very complex they will be broken down into simple intermediate goals or approxima-tions of the desired behaviour. As with most forms of therapy, trust and warmth between the therapist and child will be im-portant and the need for a clear understanding of the treatment method by all staff who are to be involved, however indirectly, will be assumed.

BEHAVIOUR THERAPY FOR THE RESIDENTIAL
COMMUNITY AS A WHOLE

In some residential communities the whole way of life is
organized around the central theme of operant conditioning
paired, sometimes, with modelling, relaxation, or systematic desensitization. As the whole day and week of the children are
within the control of the staff and can be manipulated therapeutically, a residential community would appear to be ideally
suited to the use of operant conditioning. I am not suggesting that
the community should become one gigantic Skinner Box where
the children metaphorically have to press a bar for every right and
privilege but the range of possible reinforcers and rewards is
wider and more flexible than in a situation where the therapist
only comes into contact with the child for a short time each week.

The possible disadvantage of organizing an entire community
on behaviourist principles is that children coming into the community have to be fitted into an existing system as opposed to
the system fitting round them. Selection of the children who
might be suitably placed in a residential community which
employs only behaviour modification must be based on a sound
assessment that the child's major problems have arisen from
learnt maladaptive behaviours which may be amenable to a
process of 'un-learning' or modification.

If too many children with the same problem are introduced
into the community there will be little opportunity for them to
model on the more desirable behaviour of children without that
particular problem and a child's peer group may spontaneously
reinforce the behaviour which the therapist is endeavouring to
change.

As the children will be thrown into a situation where all the
other members of the community will be involved directly and
indirectly in each other's personal therapy, it is wise to choose
children with at least some small capacity to make relationships
and some capacity to be consciously involved in their own treatment.

Selection of staff to work in this type of community is also of
vital importance as behaviour modification programmes require

staff who find no difficulty in being consistent and highly structured in their work and can retain some degree of objectivity in their monitoring and recording of behaviour.

A residential community organized entirely on behaviourist principles usually operates what has been named 'a token economy'. This system is called an economy because it deals in 'payment' for specified desirable behaviours and in many ways mirrors the larger society outside the residential community. The three major characteristics of a token economy are: (1) behaviours identified as essential for the day-to-day running of the community, e.g. co-operation with staff and peers, use of initiative, some degree of self-management and mutual support, appropriate social behaviour, are identified and designated by staff as behaviours which can be reinforced; (2) a type of currency, i.e. 'tokens', which can be traded in for a variety of material rewards or privileges can be earned by the performance of the specified desired behaviours; (3) an exchange system in which a specified number of tokens can be used to purchase the rewards and privileges offered is devised.

If we refer back to the discussion of operant conditioning in the previous chapter (p. 114) it can be seen that the basic principles of successful operant conditioning can readily be applied to the organization of group therapy through the use of a token economy in a residential community. The organization of the entire community on a behaviour group therapy model will be discussed under the following headings:

(1) Behaviours to be changed
(2) Operant conditioning − a group approach
(3) Selection and scheduling of positive reinforcers
(4) Extinction
(5) Time out and punishment
(6) Modelling
(7) Recording and monitoring progress
(8) The weaning process.

**Behaviours to be changed**

When a child enters a residential community he is entering a society and sub-culture which is very different from the small family culture from which he has come — however small the residential community. He is also entering an 'institution' — however non-institutional the community is striving to be. Even in the smallest, most homely residential community there are likely to be more children, more parent/authority figures who are not always present, and more structured and explicit rules and demands on behaviour than would be likely to be found in the child's family setting. A certain amount of institutionalization and the depersonalization which goes with it is bound to take place.

When residential therapists begin to consider which behaviours they will aim to modify, they must bear in mind the temptation to select only the behaviours which are considered desirable for the smooth running of the institution. Such behaviours may be highly relevant to the child's existence within the residential community but totally irrelevant to his home situation or to the wider community outside the institution. For instance, a child who comes from a one-parent family, where that one parent is perhaps physically or mentally ill, may need to develop a high degree of self-reliance, an ability to use initiative and a capacity for self-regulation. The residential community in order to run smoothly may encourage children to become dependent, conforming, and unquestioning of authority and happy to have each facet of daily life, e.g. personal hygiene, bed-times, meals, regulated by staff.

When selecting the behaviour changes which will constitute the treatment goals for a child, it is important to relate them to the child's own background and to tailor them to the social roles and competencies which he is going to need in order to adjust happily within his own family as well as within the community at large. The residential therapist must try to create some situations within the residential community which simulate the wider society to which the child will be returned. For instance, if a child is to return home to a situation where he will be expected to help with the responsibility for younger siblings, it would be helpful to put him in situations within the residential community where he can learn to take some responsibility for younger children. A child may be returning to a home where, because of parental inadequacy, he may have to bear the major responsibility for managing the money. If, within the residential community, he is never allowed to budget for himself, shop to look for competitive prices or taught to save for emergencies or special occasions, he will not have learnt the skills which will be vital to him when he returns home.

Behaviours to be changed therefore will fit into two main categories: (1) behaviours which are desirable for the smooth and happy running of the residential community; and (2) behaviours which the child will need in order to survive happily within his own home. Hopefully, many of the behaviour changes desired in the first category will coincide with the changes desired in the second category but it is sometimes difficult for staff to believe that the child who has learnt to live successfully in a residential community may not be able to transfer these skills to a vastly different home environment. When selecting behaviours to be modified, therefore, it is important to have discussed with the child's parents and family how they see the need for change and in what circumstances the 'problem' behaviour manifests itself at home.

Once a child has been admitted to a residential community which is organized as a token economy, there will be a period of assessment during which time observation and recording of the frequency and intensity of his problem behaviours will take place in order to determine a base line. Methods of obtaining a base line are described in Chapter 4, page 105. The important point when choosing which specific behaviours to observe and record is to make sure that all staff concerned in the treatment programme define identified problems in the child in a similar way. Poteet (1973) describes an experiment in which a group of teachers was asked to define certain words which describe undesirable behaviours. The results are set out in *Table 5(1)*. Each word conveyed a slightly different meaning to each teacher and would be linked with a slightly different set of behaviours.

Clearly, staff in a token economy system must get together and discuss and specify the target behaviour changes for each

TABLE 5(1) *Teachers' definitions of words describing undesirable behaviour*

| Noisy | Loud | Disrespectful | On the go |
|---|---|---|---|
| rattles paper | speaks out | sasses | very active |
| not sure of self | boyish | mouthy | can't sit still |
| bored | drops things | doesn't listen | discontented |
| wants attention | wants attention | attention-seeking | work is too hard |
| lacks self-respect | hostile | resentment | feels inadequate |
| thumps desk | spoiled | hyperactive | hyperactive |

child in a language which ensures that, in their observations, all staff involved are looking for and describing the same thing.

The range of behaviours which are likely to be amenable to behaviour modification is vast (see p. 99). Selection of the most vital behaviour changes to be desired and the construction of a hierarchy of changes from the least important to the most important should take place during the assessment period and before the child enters the token system.

When base lines have been obtained the goals will fall into two broad categories: (1) problem behaviour which needs to be reduced or eliminated; (2) good or potentially good behaviour which needs to be developed. The goals for each child should be discussed with the child and staff and written down. Ideally, these goals will be expressed in a positive form which emphasizes the increase of desirable behaviour as opposed to emphasizing the decrease of undesirable behaviour, see *Table 5(2)*. Making a deliberate point of expressing goals positively

TABLE 5(2) *Negatively and positively exposed behavioural goals*

| Negatively expressed behavioural goal | Positively expressed behavioural goal |
|---|---|
| (1)  Stop bullying younger children | Be gentle and non-aggressive in behaviour towards younger children |
| (2)  Stop swearing | Use acceptable language |
| (3)  Stop withdrawing from other children | Play with at least one other child each day |

may seem somewhat artificial but it is important in that it helps the child and therapist alike to look at the child's potential for desirable behaviour as opposed to concentrating on his present undesirable and problem behaviour.

I would stress again that behaviour modification within a token economy system should not merely be an effective way of controlling problem behaviour but should be used to develop the children's potential strengths and abilities.

## Operant conditioning – a group approach

In some residential communities the token economy is administered solely by staff who make all the decisions concerning treatment goals, agents of reinforcements, schedules of reinforcement. It is possible, however, to organize the token economy on a·group model which uses the combined resources of children and staff to modify individual and group behaviour. This can be achieved most effectively through a daily meeting of the whole community at which responsibility for evaluating and modifying the behaviour of each child, and for deciding how the tokens should be given, is delegated to the group. Staff do not opt out of all responsibility in this approach but are there to advise and enable the group to arrive at constructive decisions.

Children and staff involved in the daily meeting will have two main functions: (1) to identify a behaviour or set of behaviours on which each child is prepared to work; and (2) to assess and monitor progress.

The leader may, in turn, give each child the opportunity to express what he feels about his own behaviour and which behaviours he would like to change and then ask for suggestions from the group as to how these changes could be achieved. The agreed goals for each child should be written down and at the next meeting the group would be asked to comment on the progress of each individual and to offer support, advice, and constructive criticism and help in the setting of new goals.

The use of peer group pressure, as opposed to staff domination to eliminate undesirable behaviour and enhance desirable behaviour can be most effective provided that the staff involved are aware of and in a position to manipulate the dynamics of the group. All groups will have a pecking order in which the child with the highest status amongst his peers is highly influential. Staff can exploit this influence constructively by using the children's group leader as a satisfactory model. In order to ensure that the model is modelling predominantly desirable behaviours, the desirable behaviours which he displays should be heavily rewarded by staff and be seen to be heavily rewarded by the other children.

At the bottom of the pecking order will be the child with the lowest status and possibly the most problems – certainly in relation to his peer group. To ensure that this child does not become the group scapegoat on to whom the rest of the group can project their own problems and see them punished vicariously through the lack of approval which the scapegoat child attracts, staff must work hard to find ways in which that child also can be heavily rewarded for any behaviour or approximation of a behaviour which is desirable.

If the residential community is a happy cohesive group in which members can invest heavily and can confidently expect to have their needs met, a new child entering the community will raidly respond to group approval or disapproval and in this way the whole group, as opposed to the staff group alone, will constitute a powerful agent of reinforcement which, if channelled constructively, will facilitate the development of desirable behaviours.

**Selection and scheduling of positive reinforcers**

Although most of the techniques associated with behaviour therapy will be employed in the running of a token economy, the use of positive reinforcement will be the most important. Having identified the behaviours which cause a child to have problems of adjustment and defined the desired changes in these behaviours in a way which allows for accurate observation and recording of behaviour and behaviour change, the therapist's next step is to identify, firstly, the agents of reinforcement through which the undesirable behaviour was previously maintained and, secondly, the exact forms of positive reinforcement which are likely to be successful in producing desirable behaviour.

The most common form of positive reinforcement of undesirable behaviour experienced by children before they come into a residential community is the attention which this undesirable behaviour has attracted to them. This applies equally to the aggressive or delinquent child who will certainly have attracted a great deal of attention and to the withdrawn over-anxious child who has been 'a worry' to his parents and teachers. As attention is what most of our children are seeking, it is obviously going to constitute a valuable means of positively reinforcing children's behaviour when they are in a residential community. The difference will be that attention will be given increasingly for desirable behaviour and decreasingly for undesirable behaviour.

In the early stages when a child first enters a token economy the most effective reinforcers of desirable behaviour will be tokens which can be traded in for material rewards or privileges paired with praise. In order to determine which particular rewards and privileges provide a real incentive for the child to produce desirable behaviour, the therapist can use a short questionnaire, administered verbally or in written form, to gain some clues to the child's inner concept of what constitutes a reward to him. The questionnaire might read something like that in *Figure 5(1)*.

Once the therapist has collected suggestions for suitable rewards from the individuals in the group, these can be presented in the form of a menu for the day or week. The group, in group discussion at the daily meeting, will decide how many tokens they think should be earned and traded in for each reward. A menu of the week in a residential community which caters for children between the ages of eight and sixteen could look something like that in *Table 5(3)*.

We have found that a simple way to calculate how many tokens should be required to trade in for a material reward is to give each token a monetary value, e.g. 2p. Thus skating, which is an expensive outing, would cost 100 tokens.

Some children will prefer to collect tokens for highly personal

*Figure 5(1)* Questionnaire to discover each child's preferred reward system

---

(a) If you could go into a toy or game shop and choose any six small games to the value of about £1 each, which would you choose?

| | |
|---|---|
| (1) | (4) |
| (2) | (5) |
| (3) | (6) |

(b) If you could choose time to spend on your own with one particular adult in the residential community, whom would you choose?

(1) houseparent
(2) teacher
(3) social worker
(4) psychologist
(5) head of the community
(6) cook
(7) cleaner
(8) caretaker

(The above list would be matched with staff who are available to give time to children and are part of the residential community.)

(c) If you could choose a privilege as a reward, which of the following might you choose?

(1) Staying up late.
(2) Missing a lesson or chore.
(3) Going out to the cinema, skating, etc.
(4) Spending time alone.
(5) Inviting a friend to tea or supper.
(6) Taking a trip to the local shops.

(The lists of possible rewards would, of course, be dependent on the location and staffing of the residential community and lists of possible rewards would be compiled with these in mind.)

---

rewards and the number of tokens required for these will be negotiated in the group meeting and agreed to by the child and staff concerned, e.g. a child who has a particular hobby like bird-watching may decide to save tokens to the value of an expedition to a bird sanctuary. There is much scope for imagination on the part of staff and children when deciding on the menu for the day or week and as the children develop new interests new rewards will be added to the menu.

TABLE 5(3) *'Menu' of the week*

| | Tokens |
|---|---|
| Going to bed half an hour later than usual | 10 |
| Not having to wash up for a day | 10 |
| Receiving a bag of sweets | 20 |
| Taking a bus to the local shops | 20 |
| Going out with favourite adult | 40 |
| Going to the cinema | 50 |
| Receiving a tennis ball | 40 |
| Inviting a friend to supper | 20 |
| Buying a favourite game or toy to the value of £1 | 60 |
| Going ice-skating | 100 |

During the early stages of a child's life within a token economy, it will be essential to reinforce the desired target behaviour by giving tokens, whenever it occurs, in order to establish a pattern of stimulus and rewarding response. It may be necessary to provide small 'cheap' rewards for which tokens can be traded in at very short time intervals. Once an individual child has established himself within the token economy, it will be necessary to vary the schedule of reinforcement. If we refer back to our discussion of schedules of reinforcement (p. 135) we recall that schedules of reinforcement which no longer reward every time the behaviour occurs can either be organized on a fixed or variable ratio schedule or on a fixed or variable interval schedule.

If a child moves onto a fixed ratio schedule he will be rewarded after he has given a specified number of desirable behaviour responses, e.g. for every three times he helps a younger child (his target behaviour being to stop bullying) he receives ten tokens. Once he has grown accustomed to this pattern of reinforcement and is becoming a little blasé, the therapist may move onto a variable ratio schedule of reinforcement in which the child is rewarded for varying numbers of the desired response, e.g. one day he may be given tokens for offering to go to the shop for a member of staff, another time he may go three or five times before a reward is given.

When an interval schedule of reinforcement is used the child may at first be rewarded with tokens at fixed intervals, e.g.

every half an hour, during which the desirable behaviour has been observed or there has been an observable absence of an undesirable behaviour. This fixed interval schedule may later be changed to a variable interval schedule in which the child is not sure what time interval is to elapse before his next reward.

The choice of schedules will depend on the individual child, the therapist, and the environment. The important point to remember is that, to be effective, the schedule of reinforcement should be changed progressively to the point where a child is able to produce desirable behaviour in the knowledge that the behaviour may or may not be rewarded with a tangible reward but that the internalized reward of knowing he has behaved well is reward enough. When a child has established mutually rewarding relationships with peers and staff, social approval and disapproval, pride in accomplishments or pride in helping the group achieve a goal become important agents of reinforcement.

In a group approach to behaviour modification through the use of a token economy, it is sometimes helpful to pair a child who is a high token winner with a child whose achievement is low. The tokens earned by each child are pooled, then divided into two. The high achiever is motivated to encourage his partner so that his own number of tokens is not too depleted and the low achiever is spurred on to greater effort so that he does not let his partner down.

The form of token used in a residential community which operates a token economy can vary from stars on a chart to counters or cards which are marked. It is essential to choose a currency which is not easily forged! For some young children in the very early stages of behaviour modification, it may be necessary to use rewards themselves, e.g. chocolate drops, instead of a symbolic token which can be traded in later. Some children like to have a bank account in which they can store up tokens and some children like to hand their tokens in to a special member of staff for safe keeping. Whatever the particular method used it is important that it is consistent throughout the residential community and that staff reach a consensus on the pattern of rewarding and positive reinforcement to be used.

**Extinction**

Whereas the use of positive reinforcers will be the most obvious technique within a token economy, the method of diminishing an undesirable response through ignoring it will also be of value. This process is called extinction (see p. 134) and is particularly useful in helping a child to develop alternative methods of gaining attention to the anti-social methods he used previously. At its simplest level this technique consists of ignoring the undesirable behaviour, e.g. temper tantrum, and rewarding the child heavily when he displays an alternative, non-aggressive response to a stimulus which would formerly have produced a temper tantrum.

At a more sophisticated level, the behaviour group therapist may decide not only to ignore the undesirable behaviour displayed by a child but also to reward all other children in the vicinity who are not showing the same behaviour. For instance, a fight may break out between two children. Several children will be in the near vicinity and have the choice between joining in the fight or ignoring it. When the therapist arrives on the scene he may decide to ignore the two boys who are fighting and hand out tokens to all the other children who are not taking part in the fight. He may continue to hand out tokens in this way until one of the fighters at least becomes envious of his token-winning peers and decides to stop fighting.

The behaviours most amenable to extinction techniques are those which were formerly maintained through heavy positive reinforcement. For instance, a child who has repeatedly gained his parents' attention by banging his head on the wall will soon give up this piece of behaviour if no one takes any notice of him when he does it. The co-operation of all staff and peers in this planned ignoring is essential but, of course, there are certain destructive behaviours which it is impossible to ignore, e.g. a violent attack on another child. When planned ignoring of undesirable behaviour is paired with rewarding of alternative desirable behaviour, however, it can be a valuable adjunct to the use of positive reinforcement in a programme of behaviour modification.

## Time Out and punishment

The use of 'Time Out' in a token economy may at first look like the age-old habit of teachers who tell a child to 'leave the room!'. It is in fact the withdrawal of an individual child from the group but the more important feature of Time Out is that during that time the child cannot earn tokens.

It is essential to have a separate room or space to use as a Time Out room where the child will not come into contact with anyone. If, for example, he were sent to his bedroom or dormitory there may be another child, a cleaner, or another member of staff there and the child then has the opportunity of making Time Out a pleasant experience by talking to someone and receiving positive reinforcement for the behaviour for which he was sent out.

The length of time spent in the Time Out room need not be long – perhaps five minutes – as the mere removal from a situation in which the child could be earning tokens is 'punishment' enough.

Time Out is usually used as a last resort when the therapist is unable to control the positive reinforcement which a peer group may be giving to an individual child's undesirable behaviour. For example, most groups of children have one member who likes to play the clown and make the group laugh. There are times when this is highly amusing and the situation is appropriate. At other times, perhaps when the group is dealing with a serious problem or is concentrating on a task, the 'clown behaviour' is inappropriate. The rest of the children may not see, or may not want to see, the inappropriateness of the moment, and, through laughter and attention, continue to reinforce the unhelpful behaviour of the 'clown'. At this point one solution for the therapist is to send the child to Time Out where he will no longer receive reinforcement and where he will be unable to earn tokens.

Being sent to the Time Out room will undoubtedly feel like a punishment to the child concerned and most token economies would try to use it sparingly. There are occasions, however, when the careful use of punishment can be successful in reducing undesirable behaviour. Becker (1971) provides a helpful comment on the use of punishment within a behaviour modification programme:

> 'Punishment is an effective method for changing behavior. However, because the person punished may learn to avoid and escape from the punisher, this is not usually a preferred method. There are problem behaviors where the use of punishment is the most humane thing that can be done. These problems usually involve very intensive or very frequent problem behaviors. When punishment must be used, care must be taken to ensure its effectiveness and to minimize the development of avoidance behaviors.
>
> Effective Punishment:
> (1) is given immediately;
> (2) relies on withdrawal of reinforcers and provides clear steps for regaining them;
> (3) makes use of a warning signal;
> (4) is carried out in a calm, matter of fact, way;
> (5) is accompanied by much reinforcement of behavior incompatible with the behavior being punished; and
> (6) also uses procedures to make sure that undesired behaviors do not receive reinforcement.'

For Time Out to be of any significance to a child it needs to be used as a withdrawal from a situation in which the child was being heavily rewarded and, therefore, will be painfully aware of the tokens he is now unable to gain.

## Modelling

As was remarked in the previous discussion of modelling (page 120) all children model consciously and unconsciously on the behaviour and attitudes of the children and adults with whom they come into close contact. We have already touched on the importance of providing a variety of models within a residential community. Not all communities have a say in which children they will admit but wherever possible it is helpful if the group is not overbalanced by any one category of problem, e.g. delinquency or withdrawal.

In a token economy which is divided into small sub-groups, each group should contain some children who have been in the community for some time and, hopefully, can model desirable behaviours for newer children. The pairing of a high token earner with a low token earner previously mentioned is also providing the less successful child with a satisfactory model.

The therapist may introduce a child to new desirable patterns of behaviour by coupling reinforcement with modelling. Thus, when a child 'copies' a piece of constructive behaviour displayed by the model, the therapist can reinforce heavily, with tokens, both the behaviour of the model and the child who is attempting an approximation of the model's 'good' behaviour. To increase the reinforcement even further, the therapist may decide to reward the whole group when one child displays for the first time a new, helpful piece of behaviour which he has learnt by imitating other children in the group.

Sometimes it is possible to enlist the help of a high-status child in the group to encourage and teach a newer child to inhibit his destructive responses or to disinhibit his fearful or phobic responses. For instance, a child who has been unable to express himself verbally may be influenced to communicate more freely after being placed in a group where some of the children express themselves well and are rewarded for doing so. An inhibited child may similarly learn to express strong emotions through a process of vicarious identification with another child's emotional crisis and expression of it.

## Recording and monitoring progress

Behaviour therapy is based on the manipulation of observable behaviour which can be measured and recorded. If a therapist can find no way of measuring and recording a certain behaviour, then the definition of that behaviour has not been sufficiently specific.

The first step in recording, therefore, is to define the behaviours to be modified in clear, explicit form. For example, a child may be seriously lacking in self-confidence and the therapist may wish to make his treatment goal 'to increase

John's self-confidence'. This goal, however, cannot be expressed in measurable terms until the behaviours which accompany John's lack of self-confidence have been identified. Observation of John over the course of a day might reveal the following behaviours symptomatic of his lack of self-confidence:

he avoids eye contact with any adult;
he never starts a conversation;
he allows other children to order him about;
he is afraid to try and learn a new skill, e.g. swimming.

Once the lack of confidence has been broken down into small observable pieces of behaviour, the therapist, with the help of the child, his peers, and other staff, is in a position to construct a goal sheet which will then be used to monitor John's progress. Each child may have a daily goal sheet or a weekly goal sheet with spaces for each time span or day on which to record the frequency of the behaviour.

The temptation to define each goal with emphasis on what we want the child not to do, as opposed to what we would like him to do, is very real. I have seen many goal sheets used in a token economy which resemble the following:

do not swear;
do not aggravate other children;
do not wet the bed;
do not tell lies;
do not lose temper.

Quite clearly it is easier to observe a child's behaviour in terms of the behaviours which annoy us but, if the goal sheet can be worded more positively, we are at least expressing faith in the possibility of that child changing his behaviour for the better.

A typical weekly goal sheet for a hyperactive, aggressive little boy could be like that set out in *Figure 5(2)*. If a daily goal sheet is to be used, each day would be broken into intervals and the behaviour would be recorded within those intervals.

If the same goal sheet has been used over a period of time

*Figure 5(2)* Weekly goal sheet

| | |
|---|---|
| Name: | Peter |
| Age: | Nine |
| Week starting: | 10th August |

Goals:

1. To stay in bed instead of wandering about after lights out.
2. To help a younger child, whom he has previously bullied, with one task a day.

Weekly Rating:

| | Goal 1 | Goal 2 |
|---|---|---|
| *Monday* | √ | √ |
| *Tuesday* | | |
| *Wednesday* | √ | |
| *Thursday* | √ | |
| *Friday* | √ | √ |
| *Saturday* | | |
| *Sunday* | √ | √ |
| Total | 5 | 3 |

*Figure 5(3)* Graph format for recording tokens gained daily

| | Tokens | Tokens Gained Daily | | | | | | |
|---|---|---|---|---|---|---|---|---|
| Red | 100 | | | | | | | |
| Orange | 90 | | | | | | | |
| Pink | 80 | | | | | | | |
| Purple | 70 | | | | | | | |
| Blue | 60 | | | | | | | |
| Green | 50 | | | | | | | |
| Yellow | 40 | | | | | | | |
| Brown | 30 | | | | | | | |
| Turquoise | 20 | | | | | | | |
| Maroon | 10 | | | | | | | |
| | | Mon. | Tues. | Wed. | Thurs. | Fri. | Sat. | Sun. |

without the child showing any measurable progress, the therapist, child, and group should re-examine the goals with a view to simplifying them or changing them completely. A child who cannot see himself making any progress will despair and give up trying. It is better to set small, easily attainable goals initially so that he can be rapidly reinforced for any small improvement in behaviour.

*Figure 5(4)* Snakes and ladders chart for recording tokens lost and gained

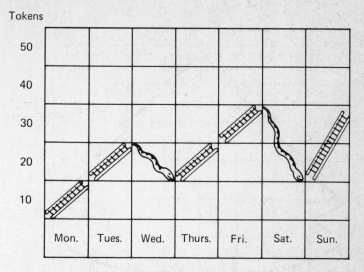

When a child is concentrating on developing one specific piece of behaviour, e.g. not wetting the bed, a small chart on his bedroom wall on which he is given a gold star for every night that he is dry can be a very simple but effective way of monitoring his progress.

There is much scope for imagination when thinking of interesting ways of charting behaviour change and the children and staff can be encouraged to use their creativity. Different colours for different numbers of tokens gained can be used to block in a graph, see *Figure 5(3)*.

When, in a token economy system, tokens are withdrawn from, as well as given to children the ups and downs of each child's personal token economy can be shown on a snakes and ladders chart; the ladders represent the number of tokens gained and accumulated over the week, the snakes show when tokens were lost, see *Figure 5(4)*.

Another way of charting the number of tokens gained, especially good for very young children, is to give each child a

*Figure 5(5)* Christmas tree chart for recording tokens lost and gained

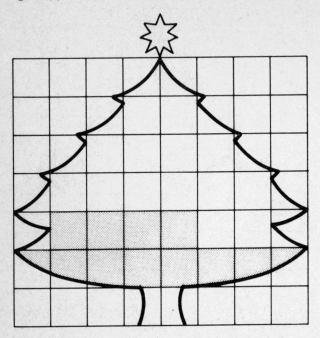

drawing of a Christmas tree on squared paper; see *Figure 5(5)*. Each square represents 2 tokens. When the tree is filled with tokens and the child has reached the star on top of the tree he is awarded a special prize.

One way of showing a cumulative total of tokens gained is to give each child a large jar into which a measure, e.g. a cupful of coloured liquid, is put into the jar for every ten tokens gained. Alternatively, the jar could be filled with coloured marbles in the same way. If the charts are fun for each child to produce, the chart itself will also become a reinforcing agent, especially if charts are on display to peers, staff, and visitors to the residential community.

To gain a complete picture of the behaviour modification programme for a child, the therapist may wish to plot a graph which shows (1) the base line; (2) the reinforcement; (3) any

*Figure 5(6)* Graph to record progress in behaviour modification

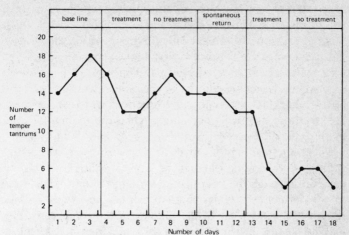

changes of behaviour when reinforcement is withdrawn; (4) any spontaneous return to previous level of desirable behaviour; (5) renewed period of reinforcement; (6) final stage of no reinforcement. (See *Figure 5(6).*) Whatever the system of recording used, each child will bring his chart to the daily or weekly meetings and his peer group will be encouraged to comment on his successes and provide helpful suggestions where he is finding the goals difficult to achieve.

Parents and teachers may also be asked to help in the recording of behaviour and will often co-operate happily in maintaining a chart when the child is at home or out at school. Again, the behaviours to be monitored must be very clearly defined and a reinforcement system compatible with that within the residential community employed. Eventually, if the behaviour modification has been successful, the child will have internalized much reinforcement and will be able to monitor and control his own behaviour in the areas which he previously found difficult.

## The weaning process

The final stage in a child's treatment within a token economy will be when he is weaned away from the use of tokens as reinforcers and he learns to produce desirable behaviour with little external reinforcement. Many children will be able to tell you themselves when they feel 'ready to come off tokens' and at this stage it is useful to have one sub-group within the residential community which is not run on a token economy. Children who have earned their way into this group are expected to regulate an increasing amount of their own behaviour and will be introduced to more and more situations which are comparable to those they will encounter beyond the residential community.

The more freedom for self-regulation at this stage the better, as this will determine whether the level of desirable behaviour achieved through the treatment programme can be transferred to a wider context. Older children can be encouraged to take responsibility for some of the running of the community, e.g. making menus, devising rotas for jobs, making rules. Membership of organizations outside the residential community, such as Scouts, Guides, Youth Clubs, Volunteer Helper Groups, provides a testing ground for the child's recently developed social competencies and ability to behave appropriately without the prop of a token system.

Rose (1973:180) has summarized the steps which are likely to result in a successful weaning away from dependency on a token economy and on the residential community as follows:

'(1) gradually increase the similarity between treatment and extra-treatment situations; (2) vary as many aspects of treatments as is organizationally feasible; (3) increase the degree of unpredictability of the treatment situation; (4) increase the degree of client responsibility; (5) increase extra group incentive; (6) encourage overlearning of the original subtasks; (7) conceptualize the learning after a variety of specific examples; and (8) prepare the client for an unsympathetic environment.'

If the treatment within a residential community which is organized as a token economy has been successful, a child will be able to transfer to his home situation and life outside the community this learning of acceptable behaviour and this should in turn help him to feel emotionally more stable and cognitively more aware of himself in relation to his environment.

## SMALL GROUP BEHAVIOUR THERAPY

Some staff groups in a residential community may not wish to organize the whole community on the behaviour therapy model we have just discussed but may feel that for one sub-group of children in particular this method has something to offer. It may be decided to hold a daily or weekly behaviour group therapy meeting with this group of children or in fact their whole day could be organized as a mini-token economy within the wider eclectically organized environment of the community. If the whole day for these children is to be organized on a behaviour therapy model, the structure of the treatment will be similar to that already discussed under token economies.

If there is to be a weekly behaviour group therapy meeting for one sub-group, it is possible to select members for that group who (a) have similar problems and are likely to benefit by a group approach to the problem or (b) need to be in a close group situation with children whose problems are varied so that they can benefit from the opportunity to model on other children and vicariously come to grips with their own problem.

Once the children for the small group therapy have been selected and meeting times and appropriate venue have been arranged, the first task of the therapist is to enable the group to become cohesive and eager to work on the task of modifying behaviour. Some of the encounter games, to be described in Chapter 8, are useful in breaking the ice in a newly formed group by crossing normal boundaries, e.g. of physical contact between staff and children, and building up warmth and trust. Once trusting relationships have developed within the group, the therapist can introduce the idea of behaviour goal sheets and ways in which the children can help each other to achieve goals.

Goal sheets are initially drawn up for each individual in the group but later some group goals may be added. The group will help in the planning of each child's goals by discussing amongst themselves and with the therapist what each child's problem

*Figure 5(7)* Example of a behaviour contract

| |
|---|
| *Name:*   Sarah (a shy, withdrawn child − friendless). |
| *Week beginning:*   10th September. |
| *Goal during the week:*   Each day I will play with one other child for at least an hour. |
| *Goal during the group meeting:*   I will offer one suggestion to help another child. |
| *Tokens to be awarded:*   Ten for each goal achieved. |
| *Signed:*   Sarah. |

behaviours appear to be. Once the goals for the week have been set, they can be written down in the form of a contract. (See *Figure 5(7)*.) This contract implies the use of tokens as a positive reinforcer of desirable behaviour but the therapist may decide to rely solely on his own and the child's peer group approval as agents of reinforcement. Whatever method of reinforcement is chosen each child should be rewarded promptly and frequently in the early stages of his behaviour modification as a prelude to the use of more varied schedules of reinforcement.

At the group meeting each child will produce his previous week's contract and in turn the other members of the group will comment on how successful, from their observations during the week, a child has been in attaining his goals. Each of his peers, plus the therapist, may award anything up to 5 points for success, which can then be converted into tokens. A weekly record sheet might look like *Figure 5(8)*. A child may keep the same goal sheet for several weeks until he and the group decide that a satisfactory level of achievement has been reached or that the goals were unrealistic and should be changed.

The group, as well as helping individuals to decide on behavioural goals and ways of achieving them, may also set itself a group task or goal. This could be in the nature of a team effort to do something for the residential community, e.g. keeping the building tidy, re-decorating a room or organizing a play scheme for younger children. Each member of the group would be given different tasks related to the desirable behaviours he normally found difficult, e.g. co-operating with other children or taking direction from staff. Rewards for this type of group behaviour

*Figure 5(8)* Example of a weekly behaviour record chart

| | | | | | | | |
|---|---|---|---|---|---|---|---|
| *Name:* Paul | | | | | | | |
| *Goal:* I will help a younger child five times each day. | | | | | | | |
| *Rate of achievement observed by:* | | | | | | | |
| John | 4 | 3 | 4 | 5 | 3 | 2 | 4 |
| Peter | 2 | 3 | 4 | 2 | 2 | 1 | 5 |
| Frank | 1 | 3 | 2 | 2 | 3 | 2 | 2 |
| Betty | 0 | 1 | 0 | 4 | 4 | 3 | 2 |
| Jane | 3 | 5 | 3 | 1 | 4 | 2 | 1 |
| Charles | 3 | 0 | 1 | 2 | 1 | 4 | 2 |
| Moira | 1 | 2 | 1 | 1 | 0 | 5 | 3 |
| Therapist | 1 | 1 | 4 | 3 | 2 | 1 | 1 |
| | Mon. | Tues. | Wed. | Thurs. | Fri. | Sat. | Sun. |
| Total out of possible 40 | 15 | 18 | 19 | 20 | 19 | 20 | 20 |
| Grand Total for week 131 out of *280* | | | | | | | |

would depend on the collective success of the members of the group and could take the form of a group outing, e.g. to the cinema, or a piece of equipment to be enjoyed by the group, e.g. a record player.

The small group meeting is the ideal setting for children to practise modelling. The therapist may choose to pair each child with a partner who has some of the behaviours each is trying to develop. For instance, each pair of children may be asked to complete a task within the group meeting which requires both imaginative, creative, and confident flair coupled with the ability to concentrate on a task for a fair length of time. If the therapist has paired the children so that a more extrovert, uninhibited, and creative child who lacks the ability to concentrate for any length of time is paired with a more introvert child whose creativity is less but whose capacity to concentrate is high, each child has the opportunity to develop, through imitation, the strengths of his partner.

Role play within a small therapy group can also be used as a modelling experience. Each child in turn is asked to describe a situation in which he frequently finds himself in trouble and which causes him problems, e.g. if he comes in late in the evening his mother defends him from his father, who is furious and becomes violent with both the mother and the child. The group is then asked to act out this scene in such a way that possible solutions are explored and the child who is watching the enactment of his problem can model an alternative behaviour to his usual response, which is to become violent himself.

Another way in which children can be helped to rehearse new desirable behaviour through role play is when the therapist, in the group meeting, asks the children to create and act a play which typifies a problem situation they are familiar with either in their own homes or in the residential community. Having decided on the plot and the characters involved, the therapist then assigns a role to each child — being careful to select roles which are contrary to the expected. Thus the child who has the lowest status in the group may be asked to play the 'hero' and the child who is the group bully may play the scapegoat.

Children who experience high anxiety over certain facets of their life can be helped in a small group meeting through programmes of relaxation. When a child expresses a chronic anxiety over a particular piece of behaviour, e.g. going swimming or taking a bus ride, the therapist can ask the group to help this child to overcome the anxiety.

The first step is to train the members of the group to relax completely. The following instructions (Rose 1973:129) can be used in teaching groups of children to relax. The therapist will put the instructions in language suited to the age of the children in the group:

'Lie on the back with feet separated slightly and arms, palms up, near the body, head centered. Bring your attention into the right arm. Try to feel the muscles and then gently but deliberately tense the muscles in that arm. Slowly increase the tension until maximum tension is reached from the hand to the top of the shoulder. Stretch the arm but don't lift it, as you will then tense other muscles. Keep your attention on the arm and don't allow any other thought to enter your mind. Remain this way for five seconds. Slowly release the tension and be as aware as possible of what is happening in the arm: that the tension is leaving it, that the form of the arm is being dissolved, as it were, that only the mass remains and that it feels very heavy. Do the same with left arm. Next the right leg. Push the heel away and pull the toes toward you in order to avoid a foot cramp. Slowly increase tension until the maximum has been reached, from the foot to the thigh. Stretch the leg but do not lift it. Again, your attention is solely directed to the leg. Remain this way five seconds. Now slowly release the tension, feeling the tension leave, the form of the leg dissolve and the mass lying heavy on the ground. Do same with other leg. Now turn your attention to the pelvic girdle. To tense this area we contract the abdominal muscles and draw them slightly upwards. Then the buttocks are drawn towards one another. Forget the rest of the body, only feel the tensed area. Slowly release the muscles of abdomen and buttocks and leave the pelvic area resting heavy on the ground. Direct your attention next to the chest box. Here tense the muscles of the chest; move the shoulders towards each other from behind, tense the back and rib muscles. Proceed as above. Bring your attention to the neck. To tense it we pull the back of the head toward the nape of the neck; hold it a few seconds and slowly let it loose. Feel the difference between the tensed neck and the neck resting on the mat. Next the muscles of the face. Clench the jaws together; tense cheeks, mouth, eyelids; wrinkle the forehead. One by one realise the tension in each of these. Let the muscles submit to the attraction of the earth. Let the lower jaw and cheeks feel the pull of gravity; the lips part slightly. Now start at the feet and work your way up to the head, feeling the heaviness in the different parts of the body. The feeling of heaviness is a first sign of a good relaxation. Feel the heaviness in the blood and every fiber of the body. Let the trunk sink even more . . . into the mat. Don't move anything. . . . You are completely relaxed, but you are also completely conscious and aware of the relaxation at the same time. Let the mind wander through the body to check whether anything more needs to be relaxed, if the body can sink still more into the mat. Remain this way for five minutes. After a certain time you will have the impression of floating outside your body. This is a successful relaxation. Don't jump up and run off. Slowly move your limbs and stretch and yawn. Increase the depth of the breathing (which becomes almost unnoticeable during the relaxing exercise), roll onto one side, stretch some more, and slowly sit up.

In addition tokens may be given in the initial phase for periods where no laughter, giggling, or horseplay occur. Furthermore, stress is placed not on being relaxed but on giving external signs of relaxation. This impression is measured by a fellow client who ascertains the degree of relaxation (being quiet, not moving, shallow breathing, loose hands, facial expressions). If these indications are present, the client is reinforced.'[1]

Once the members of the group have learnt to relax, the therapist can ask the child whose problems are in focus during that meeting to arrange his anxieties in a hierarchy ranging from the least anxiety provoking to the most. For instance, if a child experiences chronic anxiety over going to school his anxiety hierarchy might be:

(1) Getting out of bed on a school morning.
(2) Putting on school uniform.
(3) Leaving the house to go to school.
(4) Leaving mother at home.
(5) Walking along the road to school.
(6) Entering the school gates.
(7) Entering the school.
(8) Entering own classroom.

Having established this hierarchy the therapist then asks each member of the group to relax, through the techniques described, and proceeds to ask the group to imagine they are taking, in turn, the eight steps to going to school outlined above. Each hierarchy is then further developed by describing to the child situations which have elements in common with the first theme, i.e. going to school, which might also cause acute anxiety. These might include going to the shops alone, going to a place of public entertainment, e.g. cinema or theatre, going to

---

[1] Extract reproduced by permission of the publishers.

a strange hotel on holiday, staying away from home with friends or relatives. Repeated vicarious rehearsals of these anxiety-provoking situations by helping the child to imagine them while he is in a state of complete relaxation will gradually have the effect of diminishing the fear response when the actual anxiety-provoking stimulus is presented.

This form of group systematic desensitization is particularly useful when the children in the group have similar anxieties but can also be of value in helping a particular child through the technique which is strengthened by the participation of the child's peers.

Monitoring of behaviour and recording of behaviour change can be done in small groups in ways similar to those employed in large group therapy. The final stage for each child in the small group will be when he has come to terms with his problems and is producing, on a regular basis, the desired behaviour he identified when setting his treatment goals. He may then be 'promoted' out of the behaviour therapy group and encouraged to integrate into the wider group of the residential community.

SUMMARY

In this chapter the use of behaviour modification and behaviour therapy in a residential community has been discussed. Techniques for organizing the whole community on a token economy system were examined and adaptations of the key behaviourist concepts of operant conditioning, extinction, modelling, and systematic desensitization to large or small group therapy were explored. The importance of approaching behaviour change positively and of specifying goals in terms of observable behaviour was stressed.

# 6 Encounter Group Theory

'Encounter' is an umbrella term I am using to describe a movement in psychology and psychotherapy which basically grew out of, and away from, a psycho-analytic view of human personality. A group of psychologists who wished to explore a less pessimistic and determinist view of personality development than Freud and his followers had proposed began to explore ways of defining and enhancing man's potential for self-actualization. For some of them, e.g. Carl Rogers, the starting point was to investigate, and try to help, people who suffered from neuroses and an inability to realize their potential for leading an emotionally and intellectually satisfying life. For others, like Maslow, the starting point was to investigate, and try to identify, the qualities of people who had successfully come to terms with themselves in relation to others and who were engaged in reaching their full potential as human beings. The basic assumption that they held in common was that the exploration and expression of feelings and emotions were more important in determining personality and its contingent behaviours than a reflection on the origins of these feelings or an assumption that all behaviour is 'learnt' in the behaviourist sense of the word.

The Esalen Institute at Big Sur, California, became the international centre for people seeking to widen their view of human experience and the home of encounter groups, gestalt therapy, Rogerian psychotherapy, bioenergetics, meditation, zen, yoga and other existentialist philosophies. This movement stressed the possibility of change for the better and man's ability to transform his own life, through communication and interaction with other people in a therapeutic dyad or group. In this sense, encounter group theory has much to offer the residential therapist in the way of understanding himself and the children with whom he works.

In this chapter we will examine some of the concepts explored by Abraham Maslow, Carl Rogers, Fritz Perls, Jacob Moreno, and Arthur Janov as a basis for organizing encounter group therapy to be discussed in Chapter 7.

## ABRAHAM MASLOW

I have chosen to write about Maslow first because, in a sense, his analysis of human needs and the process of self-actualization form the basis, however implicit, of most of the humanistic experiential concepts of desired change and development within both the healthy and the unhealthy personality.

Although Maslow's early training was heavily influenced by the behaviourist Watson and the psychologist Harlow, he identified the three most important influential factors in his life as (1) getting married, (2) becoming a father, and (3) the opportunity to model on great teachers such as neo-Freudians Erich and Karen Horney, the anthropologist Ruth Benedict, and the gestalt psychologist Max Wertheimer. Study of these models led him to seek a definition of the heights to which human beings can aspire as opposed to the examination, conducted by many of his contemporaries, of the depths of despair and the neuroses to which man can sink. Maslow's main goal became to discover what was man's potential for full human development and expression. His basic assumption was that all human beings have an innate drive towards self-fulfilment or 'self-actualization'. Although he would not deny that poor childhood experiences can arrest this process of self-actualization, he firmly believed in the possibility of overcoming early crippling experiences and discovering new potential for self-fulfilment. His philosophy, therefore, is one which is eminently suited to residential social workers who are frequently faced with children who clearly are not realizing their full potential either emotionally, intellectually and, sometimes, even physically.

In *Toward a Psychology of Being* (1968), Maslow put forward his theory of human needs. These, he maintained, are arranged in a hierarchy from strongest to weakest and must be satisfied in that order.

## (1) Physiological needs

These are the needs which must be satisfied for the individual to survive and include food, water, air, and sleep. Until these needs are adequately met by, in our case, the provision of a secure physical environment within the residential community, where children can expect to be fed when hungry and sleep comfortably when tired, we cannot expect them to be concerned with the other needs of the hierarchy. This may seem a somewhat obvious remark to make but there are still, sadly, some residential communities in which children are punished by deprivation of food and where beds and bedrooms are not seen as places of warmth and comfort but as places of isolation and, sometimes, of punishment.

## (2) Safety needs

The second need in the hierarchy defined by Maslow is the need for security, protection, and freedom from fear and anxiety.

Most of the children coming into a residential community have not had these needs adequately met and, therefore, it is most important that the residential community is organized in such a way that each child experiences stability, order, and a certain degree of predictability within his new environment, so that his need to feel 'safe' can be met.

## (3) Belonging and love needs

When our physiological and safety needs have been met our next need is to experience a sense of belonging − to our family, the group within which we live, and our extended family, and local community. Our love needs, both giving and receiving, will be met in the context of intimate, caring relationships with those who are close to us.

In a residential community, because of the absence of immediate family, the children will look to staff to meet some of their need for love, and staff will be required not only to give love to the children in their care but also to receive it from them. If the relationships and group cohesion within the residential community are strong, each member of the community can develop a real sense of belonging and fulfil, at least to some small degree, the need to 'belong'.

## (4) Esteem needs

If a person is fortunate enough to have his three first needs met, his next drive will be to derive esteem from others and from himself. Before we can develop self-esteem we need to feel sure that we are held in esteem by others, especially those close to us whose opinions we value. Most children develop self-esteem initially through the unconditional acceptance and esteem accorded to them by their parents. Many of the children who come into a residential community have a very low feeling of self-worth. Often they blame themselves, and their lack of worth, for their present predicament and it can be very difficult to convince them that they are worthwhile people in their own right. Unless we can assure them that we genuinely hold them in esteem, they are unlikely to take the next step towards the development of self-esteem. Part of the process of gaining self-esteem is in getting to know, and to accept, one's own strengths and weaknesses and to overcome one's feelings of inferiority.

## (5) The need for self-actualization

If all the previous needs have been met at a satisfactory level, our final need will be the need for self-actualization. Schultz (1977:64) describes Maslow's concept of this need as follows:

'Self-actualization can be defined as the supreme development and use of all our abilities, the fulfilment of all our qualities and capacities. We must become what we have the potential to become. Even though the lower-order needs are satisfied — we feel secure physically and emotionally, have a sense of belonging and love, and feel ourselves to be worthy individuals — we will feel frustrated, restless, and discontent if we fail to attempt to satisfy the need for self-actualization. If that happens we will not be at peace with ourselves and cannot be described as psychologically healthy.'

As we are concerned with young, developing personalities in our residential communities we will not expect them to reach this stage of self-actualization but we may legitimately have this as our ultimate aim for each child. To acknowledge this need in ourselves as staff will be important in that it will give us greater respect for the basic needs of the children in our care and high aspirations both for ourselves and for them.

## Motivation

When discussing motivation in human behaviour, Maslow distinguished two main types which he labelled Deficiency or D-motivation and Being or B-motivation. Deficiency motivation is motivation to make up some deficiency connected with the four basic needs which precede the need for self-actualization. These deficits cause physical and psychological tension in the individual who is motivated to reduce this tension, e.g. a hungry child seeks food and an emotionally hungry child seeks security and love. The child or adult who is still working through D-needs is usually given to extremes of emotional expression, is volatile and unpredictable in his behaviour or, at the other extreme, is repressed and withdrawn.

Most of the children coming into our residential communities are governed by D-motivation and it is not until they learn to control their emotions and look on them as friends rather than enemies that their motivation reaches the Being stage.

B-motivation is associated with the self-actualization stage and is not concerned with making up deficiencies but with fulfilling potentialities and enriching and enlarging the experience of living. The person who has reached this stage of development is able to feel and express a wide range of emotions without loss of self-control and with sensitivity to the feelings of others. Life is both challenging and rewarding to this person and he is able to express himself spontaneously and joyously.

Obviously this is the state of being we would like all the children in our care to achieve and it is the ultimate, if not easily attainable, goal of most therapy. Amongst the characteristics of self-actualizers Maslow listed an efficient perception of reality, an acceptance of oneself and others, a capacity to function autonomously, a strong social awareness, a capacity for strong

TABLE 6(1) *Maslow's metaneeds and metapathologies*

| B-values | Metapathologies |
| --- | --- |
| truth | mistrust, cynicism, skepticism |
| goodness | hatred, repulsion, disgust, reliance only upon self and for self |
| beauty | vulgarity, restlessness, loss of taste, bleakness |
| unity; wholeness | disintegration |
| dichotomy-transcendence | black/white thinking, either/or thinking, simplistic view of life |
| aliveness; process | deadness, robotizing, feeling oneself to be totally determined, loss of emotion and zest in life, experiential emptiness |
| uniqueness | loss of feeling of self and individuality, feeling oneself to be interchangeable or anonymous |
| perfection | hopelessness, nothing to work for |
| necessity | chaos, unpredictability |
| completion; finality | incompleteness, hopelessness, cessation of striving and coping |
| justice | anger, cynicism, mistrust, lawlessness, total selfishness |
| order | insecurity, wariness, loss of safety and predictability, necessity for being on guard |
| simplicity | overcomplexity, confusion, bewilderment, loss of orientation |
| richness, totality, comprehensiveness | depression, uneasiness, loss of interest in the world |
| effortlessness | fatigue, strain, clumsiness, awkwardness, stiffness |
| playfulness | grimness, depression, paranoid humourlessness, loss of zest in life, cheerlessness |
| self-sufficiency | responsibility given to others |
| meaningfulness | meaninglessness, despair, senselessness of life |

interpersonal relationships and creativity coupled with a sense of humour. He described what he saw as the B-values in life and the metapathologies which arise when a person rejects or is unable to aspire to these values, see *Table 6(1)*.

Maslow's contribution to the human potential movement was significant in that it set an ideal towards which man might strive and created a belief that this ideal was attainable, at least in part, by all men. For the residential social worker the clarification of basic needs and types of motivation are helpful and the optimism of Maslow's philosophy is one which we all need to support us through therapeutic relationships with emotionally disturbed children.

## CARL ROGERS

Carl Rogers, whose concept of human development was similar in many ways to that of Maslow, arrived at this concept through a variety of influences. From a strong evangelist family, Rogers' first ambition was to become a fundamentalist Christian minister but experiences as a young man attending the World Student Christian Federation Conference in China led him to question the beliefs he had held firmly up to that point. He discarded his religious beliefs and ambitions in favour of becoming a clinical psychologist and decided to devote his life to psychotherapy. His interest in the encounter movement sprang from two sources: (1) his involvement in summer T-Group (Training Group) exercises at Bettel, Maine, where the National Training Laboratories trained managers and executives from industry in human relations skills; and (2) his contact with the Counseling Centre at the University of Chicago, where Counselors, who were to work in War Veterans' Administration Hospitals, were trained, not only to understand the problems of servicemen returning from the Second World War, but also to achieve self-understanding and an awareness of their own personal attitudes. Rogers observed that both these forms of training resulted in a deepening self-awareness and personal growth and, like Maslow, Rogers came to regard self-actualization and the realization of full potential, physically, intellectually, and emotionally, as the ultimate goal of human development.

To Rogers, the need to actualize motivates man to survive, both physically and psychologically, and is the drive behind the maturation process. Early in the maturational process the physiological and biological growth processes are the most important but gradually the emphasis shifts to the development of the personality and the goal becomes 'self-actualization'.

Attaining the goal of self-actualization will be highly influenced by childhood experiences which contribute to the growing child's concept of himself. If he receives a steady supply of what Rogers calls 'positive regard', i.e. unconditional love, the gap between his concept of himself and the self he believes he should be, the 'ideal self', will not be too great and he will grow up with a strong feeling of self-worth. If, however, like so many of our children in residential communities, this positive regard has been highly conditional, the growing child will only feel himself to be a worthwhile person under certain conditions. His self is never allowed to actualize fully because certain of its aspects must be repressed in order to ensure that he will receive at least some conditional positive regard from those close to him.

The past, however, is not an overpowering influence from which we can never escape. Rogers believes that we are guided by our own conscious perception of ourself and our world and that the present is a much more powerful influence than the past. The 'here and now' reality, which is the result of a person's unique perceptual experiences, is the soil in which our capacity to self-actualize will grow and can become more fertile through our deepening self-awareness and relationships with others.

Rogers suggests that the fully functioning and self-actualizing person will have the following five characteristics:

(1) Instead of defending himself against emotion and new experiences he will be open to a wide range of sensations, feelings, and attitudes.
(2) He will live existentially, i.e. he will live fully in every moment of existence and will be constantly influenced or inspired by each new experience.
(3) He will trust in his own feelings about what is right and which course of action he should take. If a person feels as though a certain activity is worth doing then it is worth

doing for him and he should trust his feelings more than his intellect.

(4) The healthy, self-actualizing personality will experience freedom of choice and of action and will feel that his destiny is within his own control.

(5) He will be creative and spontaneous in his behaviour with a capacity to adapt, even to traumatic experiences, and will accept new challenges with enthusiasm and confidence.

Rogers' view of man, therefore, holds out hope for change and growth and provides an optimistic framework within which to offer residential therapy. Whether the residential therapist is prepared to accept totally his concept that anyone's perception of the world is to be taken as the only right reality for him will be a highly personal decision in the face of apparent evidence from the disturbed children in the residential community that their particular 'reality' is often very negative and destructive. Some of Rogers' principles of therapy will, however, undoubtedly be of value.

### Rogers' basic encounter therapy

Rogers' form of therapy differed from traditional psycho-analytic therapy in that it placed the major responsibility for personality change on the patient or, as Rogers preferred to call him, 'the client', as opposed to the therapist. This is how his form of therapy came to be called client-centred therapy.

In a Rogerian encounter group session the leader is there to create a climate of safety which will enable members of the group to express their feelings and thoughts within the group interaction. It is important for the leader to have established a feeling of trust in the group so that members are able to express all their feelings, hostile as well as friendly, and to drop all defences in a 'here and now' experience of which the outcome is unpredictable. Rogers himself said of the group encounter, (1970:89) 'I don't know what will happen but it will be all right'. No clear distinction between growth and development goals and therapy goals is made, growth and therapy being perceived as the same thing. Honest confrontation between members of the group is encouraged in the belief that feedback about oneself, even if it is negative, can be of value in discovering one's true self. The group, if it is cohesive and has built up trust, will provide a support and sympathy to individual members and the expression of closeness, affection, and gratitude will counterbalance the expression of hostile feelings.

To facilitate the basic encounter, some Rogerian therapists use games, exercises, and role play but the central theme is always the participants' 'here-and-now' affective reactions to one another. Some of these exercises will be described in Chapter 7.

The qualities needed in a therapist who wishes to run a Rogerian encounter group have a strong emphasis on feeling. They are: (1) unconditional positive regard or warmth on the part of the therapist; (2) empathic understanding by the therapist of the client's experiences; and (3) congruence or genuineness of expression of the self in relation to the client. Therapy takes place when a person is able to get in touch with his feelings through the group interaction and as a result of feedback changes his feelings. The therapist's role is not to direct the members of the group but to facilitate healthy inter-action.

Sahakian (1965:204) summarizes the four basic premises underlying Rogers' non-directive approach to therapy:

'(1) If an individual has enough intelligence to create a problem for himself he ought to have enough to extricate himself with the aid of a counselor. (2) Not intellectual problems *per se*, but emotive and value problems lie at the root of a person's maladjustment; if these are permitted to surface, so that the individual can recognize and accept them as parts of a well-integrated personality, wholesome adjustment ensues. (3) Each individual is faced with his own peculiar problem; consequently, in treatment, no single concept, such as the Oedipus complex, will prove to be the source of all maladjustments. (4) The lack of an individualized system of values, which is acceptable to the individual as well as harmonious with the values of his society, is basic in all maladjustment.'

If, as residential therapists, we decide to adopt a Rogerian approach to helping the children in our care and we base our therapy on the principles outlined above, we must accept that the significant factor which affects each child is not reality as such, or reality as we perceive it, but reality as it is perceived by the child. The accurate empathy which enables a member of staff to understand the child's perception of reality, however distorted that perception may seem, is not always easy to achieve but is the essential starting point from which the therapist can begin to help the child to effect change and move towards an individualized system of values which is acceptable to himself as well as to the residential community and wider society in which he lives.

FRITZ PERLS

One of the most flamboyant of the psychologists who became part of the humanistic experiential encounter movement was Fritz Perls. Originally a psycho-analyst from South Africa, Perls, after a long-awaited meeting with Freud rejected him and his ideas on psycho-analysis, turned away from psycho-analysis to formulate and preach his own brand of psychotherapy, closely identified with the work of the Esalen Institute in California. His concept of personality development grew out of his understanding of the word 'gestalt', although in fact he had very little to do with the gestalt psychologists, like Max Wertheimer, *per se*. The word 'gestalt' implies a wholeness and completeness and Perls used it to describe his concept of all human functioning, which is that every organism tends towards wholeness or completion. Anything which prevents this wholeness leads to a feeling of 'unfinished business' and a person's motivation in life is to complete these incomplete gestalts in the order of their importance. The most urgent unfinished business controls our behaviour until it is satisfied and then the person goes on to deal with the next most urgent (Perls 1974).

Perls gave the example of the occasion when a fire broke out while he was giving a lecture. At that moment the fire became the most urgent business and more important than Perls' lecture. People running away from the fire grew out of breath and the need to slow down and take in more oxygen quickly followed as the most urgent need and one which had to be met before life could continue.

Perls maintained that for our psychological health we must be aware not only of our incomplete gestalts, i.e. unfinished situations, but also of our impulses and yearnings, of our resentments and particularly of the 'here and now'.

The healthy personality lives in the present and, although he does not totally ignore the future, he does not waste energy on what might happen tomorrow. It is equally non-productive to hark back continually to the past and, for example, blame our parents for everything that has gone wrong in our lives. The aim of Perls' therapy is to help people to take responsibility for their own lives and to avoid projecting, onto other people, their own inadequacies and unfulfilled desires. In order to complete our unfinished situations from the past we must be aware of them, but we cannot live in them.

This aspect of Perls' philosophy seems most apt for the children in our residential communities. They come to us usually with a great deal of 'unfinished business', parents who have apparently abandoned them, childhood longings for security unfulfilled, and it is one of our tasks as residential therapists to help these children towards a sense of wholeness within their experience of childhood.

Perls does not use the term 'self-actualization' in his writings about personality development but he does describe the ideal of maturation as the capacity to be self-regulated as opposed to externally regulated. Perls called external controls, which we internalize through our childhood experiences of control, 'top dog' because they dictate to us what we should be like and the way in which we should behave. He also identified an opposite force which he christened the 'under-dog'. The under-dog is more subtle than the top-dog in its manipulation and is the part of the personality which becomes defensive and apologetic saying, e.g. 'I try my best — I can't help it if I fail . . . I have such good intentions' (Perls 1969:19).

Perls maintains that too many people try to live up to an image of themselves which is an impossible ideal and therefore they are destined to a life of frustration and inability to actualize their true self. The concept of 'doing one's own thing' mirrored and influenced the particular society in which Perls operated, the 1960s and early 1970s in America, and was summed up by him in his 'gestalt prayer' (1969:4):

'I do my thing and you do your thing.
I am not in this world to live up to your expectations.
And you are not in this world to live up to mine.
  You are you and I am I,
And if by chance we find each other, it's beautiful.
  If not it can't be helped.'

To Perls the person who achieves a psychologically healthy way of living will have the following characteristics:

(1) He will live in the here and now and be firmly grounded in the present moment of existence.
(2) He will not suffer from overwhelming guilt but will be able to express impulses and desires openly.
(3) He will accept himself for what he is, fully aware of his own strengths and weaknesses, and will take responsibility for his own life.
(4) He will be in touch with himself as well as with those around him.
(5) He will be free of external regulation.

To residential therapists who are faced all too often with difficult, unhappy children bent on 'doing their own thing' Perls' theory of personality may appear to have little to offer. At first glance it seems to advocate a self-indulgence and freedom to express feelings, however destructive, although he does emphasize that this self-regulation should be founded on a sound knowledge of self and ability to look honestly at one's vices as well as one's virtues.

The concept of 'unfinished business' which must be completed for satisfactory personality development, however, is extremely helpful when planning therapy for children in residential communities and the insistence that the present is of more importance than an unhappy past or an uncertain future can give encouragement to the residential therapist.

**Perls' encounter group therapy**

In an encounter group run on Fritz Perls' model one person in the group usually volunteers to be in the 'hot-seat' and to work with the therapist directly, the rest of the group acting as an empathic sounding board or as participants in games and exercises which will help the person in the hot seat to get more in touch with his feelings. In the course of one group therapy meeting five or six individuals may occupy the hot seat in turn.

During the session, attention is continually drawn to the nonverbal communication which is taking place. Body language is important: 'What are your hands saying?' – 'Notice that cutting motion you are doing with your arm!' – someone frowning while he is ostensibly making a kind remark to someone else – all these non-verbal cues to what a person is really feeling are noticed and remarked upon by the therapist in order to make the group focus on what is happening here and now.

Levitsky and Perls (1972) identify several basic rules which operate in a gestalt group therapy session.

*(1) The principle of the 'now'*

Awareness in the group is concentrated on feelings which are taking place in the group at that moment in time. 'What' and 'how' are more important than 'why'. To encourage awareness of what is happening at that moment, the therapist will ask members of the group to communicate in the present tense – 'What do you feel at this moment?' If a group member needs to bring into the interaction events or feelings from his past, he is asked to enact them as if they were happening 'now'.

*(2) 'I' and 'thou'*

In order to illustrate how true communication involves both the giver and the receiver of a message, group members are asked to put all questions directly to another person, using his name instead of addressing a question to the group as a whole or talking in the abstract.

### (3) 'It' language and 'I' language

By using the word 'I' when we are talking about part of ourselves instead of the word 'it' we learn to identify and take responsibility for the behaviour in question and to see ourselves as actively involved in what happens to us,

Therapist:        'What do you feel in your throat?'
Group member: 'It is choked.'
Therapist:        'Say I am choked.'
Group member: 'I am choked.'
Therapist:        'Take that a step further.'
Group member: 'I am choking myself.'

### Use of the awareness continuum

Use of the awareness continuum is the therapist's way of leading a group member away from the 'why' of behaviour in order to concentrate on the 'how' and 'what' experience. It is Perls' way of helping you to 'lose your mind and come to your senses'. Levitsky and Perls (1972:166) quote the following interaction to illustrate the use of the awareness continuum:

'Therapist: What are you aware of now?
Patient:    Now I am aware of talking to you. I see the others in the room. I'm aware of John squirming. I can feel the tension in my shoulders. I'm aware that I get anxious as I say this.
Therapist: How do you experience the anxiety?
Patient:    I hear my voice quiver. My mouth feels dry. I talk in a very halting way.
Therapist: Are you aware of what your eyes are doing?
Patient:    Well, now I realize that my eyes keep looking away —
Therapist: Can you take responsibility for that?'

### No gossiping

Gossiping is when one member of the group talks about another as if he weren't there, e.g. 'The trouble with John is he's got a chip on his shoulder'. The therapist would then ask the speaker to address John directly — 'John, you've got a chip on your shoulder!' The no-gossiping rule is designed to stop people avoiding their feelings and to help them to express and take responsibility for what they feel.

## Asking questions

When a member of a gestalt therapy group asks a question, the therapist will pay great attention to it to ascertain whether it is really a question seeking an answer or a means of cajoling the group into seeing something in the same way as the questioner, e.g. 'Don't you think we would be better not to discuss that issue?' The questioner will then be asked to rephrase that question as a statement for which he takes responsibility — 'I do not want to discuss that issue'.

## Stay with that feeling

When a member of the group reveals that he is experiencing painful emotions in relation to something which is happening in the group or to some evocation of past trauma, the therapist may ask him to 'stay with that feeling'. He will be asked, 'What are your sensations?' 'What are your perceptions, fantasies, expectancies?' By staying with the feeling, which he has previously avoided whenever it occurred, and working through the differences between what he imagines and what is actually perceptible, the person is able to overcome his phobia over that particular subject.

Most gestalt therapists use games and exercises to help the group to get in touch with their feelings and bring to the surface repressed fears and wishes. These will be discussed in detail in Chapter 7 in relation to encounter group therapy generally.

## JACOB MORENO AND PSYCHODRAMA

Although Moreno did not propose a theory of personality, his work with groups was one of the earliest forms of group psychotherapy and many of the techniques he developed were later incorporated into different models of group therapy.

Having originally studied philosophy and medicine, Moreno developed a keen interest in the arts and drama in particular. In the 1920s he organized impromptu play groups with children in the parks of Vienna and when, in 1925, he emigrated to the United States he set up psychotherapy groups which used role-play and drama as their main techniques. He believed that by enacting the role conflicts which produced neurotic symptoms a person could, with the aid of the group, learn to approach his role conflict from a number of different angles and eventually achieve a resolution of the conflict.

In this form of group therapy the therapist acts as a director of a play. He creates a stage on which group members, in turn, can become the central figure of their own drama. They will be asked to enact several different roles from their own family drama or to play the same role in different ways. Other members of the group will be given supportive roles by the therapist or the patient and the accent on practising how it feels to be in different roles is designed to be both cathartic and instructive.

In his book *Psychodrama* (1948) Moreno introduced the use of drama as a therapeutic technique and many of the later group therapists, especially family therapists, came to regard the use of role-play as part of their stock in trade.

## ARTHUR JANOV AND PRIMAL THERAPY

Within the range of group therapies which concentrate on the release and uninhibited expression of feeling, the primal scream therapy used by Arthur Janov is perhaps the most extreme.

Janov, in his description of his theory of neurosis and its treatment (1970), states that all neurosis is an attempt to ward off emotional pain which arises from unresolved conflicts in the past. He takes the discharge of intense emotion, therefore, as the corner-stone of his therapy and he puts special emphasis on the use of the voice to express these emotions. At the beginning of a group therapy session members form a circle, hold hands, and scream. The screams may convey a variety of feeling such as anger, fear, hate, or sadness and the therapist's aim is for each member of the group to get in touch with the most hurtful feelings he has formerly repressed.

Janov also uses the gestalt technique of talking directly to a person mentioned, though not necessarily present. Janov (1970) believed that direct talk to parents especially is the main means of uncovering the emotional dynamite of primal hurt. For example, Janov describes a member of the group using direct talk to his father, who is there in imagination, saying, 'Dad, I remember how you were teaching me how to swim and you yelled at me because I was afraid to put my head under water. Finally you dunked me under.' At this point the patient might turn to the therapist with anger and say, 'Can you imagine that stupid son of a bitch dunking a six-year-old under water?' The therapist says, 'Tell him what you feel!' and he does, unloosing a tirade and screaming his fear as that six-year-old (Janov 1970:84).

The function of the other members of the group in this type of therapy is to provide a supportive framework in which the individual can safely act out these unresolved fears and hurts, over and over again if necessary.

For very disturbed children in a residential community this opportunity to express their deepest hurts in the safety of a group which cares for them may be of value provided that the therapist can then take each child on to a stage where he comes to terms with the hurt and rebuilds his life.

SUMMARY

In this chapter some of the major trends to grow out of one or more aspects of psycho-analytic psychotherapy have been examined with a view to assessing their potential value to the residential group therapist. The various new therapies which developed under the general heading of the encounter or human experiential movement were seen to have much in common in that they all emphasized the importance of getting in touch with feelings in order to effect change. From Rogers' non-directive therapy to Janov's scream therapy, the role of the therapist is seen as the catalyst in the group, enabling and facilitating the exploration and uninhibited expression of emotion. Maturity is seen as the ability to self-actualize and to reach one's full potential in all spheres of life.

# 7   Encounter Group Practice

There are almost as many models of encounter group therapy as there are therapists who run groups and the technique is wide open to adaptation and interpretation. Group therapists who take a Rogerian approach would be far less directive, for example, than a therapist who used Perls as a model.

They have many aims in common, however, and all start from the same basic assumption that the ability to express freely feelings, however ambivalent, in an ambience of trust and security, leads to greater self-acceptance and to acceptance of others. The group leader's task is to create a climate of warmth and safety and to facilitate honest communication between members of the group amongst themselves and with him.

To be effective, an encounter therapy group will not be larger than ten or twelve and, in a residential community, should include staff who work closely with the children as well as a varied cross-section of children with emotional problems. A residential community can be an ideal setting in which to run regular encounter groups, possibly weekly or twice weekly, as the members of the group will already have a vested interest in the success of the group as part of the larger group in which they are having to learn to survive.

The therapist who decides to use this form of group therapy may wish to select children for the group whose problems seem to stem mainly from unresolved emotional conflicts – in Perls' language, 'unfinished business'. The games and exercises used in encounter group therapy can also be useful in helping extremely withdrawn and inhibited children to relax and gain the confidence to express themselves freely and learn new ways of communicating.

Bearing in mind the principles of self-actualization and self-realization combined with acceptance of others, discussed in

Chapter 6, I will now outline some of the games and exercises it is possible to use in an encounter group session under the following general headings which define the aims of the exercises:

(1) Games to break down barriers, build up trust, and facilitate group cohesion.
(2) Exercises which enable the group to work on a task as a group.
(3) Exercises in communication − verbal and written.
(4) Exercises in communication − non-verbal.
(5) Increasing the awareness continuum − physically.
(6) Increasing the awareness continuum − emotionally.
(7) Unfinished business.
(8) Games to increase creativity and spontaneity, to explore fantasy, and to have fun.
(9) Role play and psychodrama.
(10) Feedback − positive and negative.

## (1) GAMES TO BREAK DOWN BARRIERS, BUILD UP TRUST, AND FACILITATE GROUP COHESION

In most therapy groups which involve adults and children there is, initially, a set of expectations about boundaries. Boundaries of physical contact, verbal expression, and non-verbal expression have usually been firmly established between children in a residential community and staff who are the authority figures. In an encounter group experience, these boundaries are no longer appropriate as the therapist is striving to encourage uninhibited communication between all members of the group, including staff, and the discovery and expression of the full range of emotions the members of the group might feel. Exercises which cut across the normal boundaries of touch and polite talk are very helpful early in the group's development. Here are some which might be helpful but no doubt the children and staff will be able to invent new games and add to this list once they have experienced the excitement of crossing normal barriers.

*Game One − milling around*
(1) Members of the group place their chairs in a circle with some space in the middle for them all to 'mill around'.

(2) All members mill around, i.e. walk round freely within the circle smiling at as many people as they can in one minute.

(3) The leader claps his hands, at which point members have to shake hands as many times as they can with people in the group for one minute.

(4) When the leader claps his hands, members pat as many people on the back as they can in one minute.

(5) When the leader claps his hands, members kiss as many people on the right cheek as they can in one minute.

(6) Members next go round the circle trying to find a partner who is their height or has the same length arms or legs, has the same eye colour or the same size feet.

(7) To finish the game, when the leader claps his hands all members pretend to throw a temper tantrum.

*Game Two – like groups*

A variation of the first game is that, when the leader claps his hands, the members of the group form into sub-groups under the following headings:

(a) first children in the family;
(b) children whose favourite game is football and those whose is cricket;
(c) those with blue eyes and those with brown;
(d) those who'd like to be cops and those who'd like to be robbers.

Any sub-groupings that might be relevant may be used.

*Game Three – getting to know names* (good for a newly formed group)

(1) The group sits in a circle.

(2) A large ball is thrown from one person to another, who must shout his name out clearly when he catches the ball.

(3) When all Christian names have been clearly heard, the rule changes so that the person who is throwing the ball calls out the name of the person to whom he is throwing it.

## Game Four – *big circle – small circle*

(1) Members stand in a circle, hold hands and make the biggest circle possible.

(2) Repeat exercise but make the smallest circle possible.

## Game Five – *human chain*

(1) Group members stand in line facing the same direction.

(2) Each person locks his arms around the person in front of him.

(3) At a given signal the whole group lies down on the floor still holding on to the person in front.

(4) The column slides across the floor by alternately moving legs and shoulders.

(5) The group attempts to stand up again without letting go.

## Game Six – *chuckle belly*

(1) In turn each person lies on the floor with his head on the tummy of the person before him, creating a zigzag line on the floor.

(2) The leader then tickles the first person so that he starts to chuckle.

(3) The chuckle is passed down the line of tummies until it reaches the last person.

## Game Seven – *Chinese fencing*

(1) Each person puts his left hand behind his back and uses his right forefinger to point, like a sword.

(2) At the leader's signal he tries to touch as many other people as possible between the shoulder-blades.

## Game Eight – *pile up*

(1) All lie on the floor on their stomachs, heads pointing inwards, as far away from the centre of the room as possible.

(2) At the leader's signal all close their eyes, and crawl forward on their stomachs until they all meet in the centre of the room and form a pile up.

*Game Nine — hot seat*

(1) Group members sit on chairs in a large enough circle to allow room for milling around.

(2) They are asked to choose a number, one or two.

(3) The leader designates one chair as the 'hot-seat'.

(4) Whoever occupies the hot seat gives a command to the group to change seats by milling round the circle and while milling to act a certain role, e.g.:

all the number ones will be ballet dancers;

all the number twos will be elephants.

(5) Whoever finishes up in the hot seat gives the next command, e.g.:

all the number ones will be pastry;

all the number twos will be rolling pins.

*Game Ten — statues*

(1) The group divides into pairs.

(2) In turn, each partner uses an imaginary tin of spray-on cement with which he covers his partner.

(3) He then moulds him into a statue which the rest of the group can come and admire.

*Game Eleven — orchestra*

(1) The group stands in a tight circle, each person with his arms round the shoulders of the two people next to him.

(2) The leader asks each person to think of the sound of a musical instrument he can imitate with his voice, e.g. drum, bugle, flute.

(3) The leader starts by making his sound.

(4) When he squeezes the shoulder of the person on his left, that person adds his sound.

(5) This continues round the circle until everyone is adding to the 'orchestra' and the group is swaying from side to side in rhythm.

(6) The leader stops his own sound, then squeezes the shoulder of the person on his left who then stops his sound.

(7) This continues round the circle until there is silence.

*Game Twelve — lead the band*

A variation of 'orchestra' is when one person is appointed conductor of the orchestra.

(1) The group sits in front of him and each person makes a musical sound as in the previous game.

(2) When the conductor raises his hands up high, the 'instruments' make a loud sound and when he lowers his hands they make a gentle sound.

(3) Different members of the group take turns in being the conductor.

*Game Thirteen — the ministry of funny walks*

(1) The group is divided into two groups who sit facing each other across the room.

(2) The first person on the left row walks over to his partner on the opposite side doing a 'funny walk'.

(3) His partner crosses the room towards the second person on the left row. For the first half of his walk he imitates player number one. For the second half he invents his own 'funny walk'.

(4) This continues down the lines until everyone has imitated a funny walk and invented one of his own.

*Game Fourteen — under the bridges*

(1) Group members form a circle, holding hands.

(2) One member frees one hand and leads the others 'under the bridges' of hands.

(3) The group ties itself into a knot.

*Game Fifteen — rhythm ritual*

(1) The group sits in a close circle.

(2) The leader, or one of the group, invents a rhythm, e.g. three claps, two finger clicks, pat knees once, which the group imitates in unison.

(3) The group keeps repeating the rhythm, but, in between each sequence, each member in turn answers a question set by the leader, e.g., give a sound for how you feel at this moment, say your favourite food, what frightens you, what annoys

you, where would you go on holiday, as a young child I was
. . ., etc.

## Game Sixteen — *guide-dog*

(1) The group divides into pairs.
(2) One partner is blindfolded while the other takes him round
the room introducing him to other people and objects in the
room by putting his hands on them and describing them.
(3) The partners reverse roles.

## Game Seventeen — *safety-net*

A variation of the game above.

(1) One partner is blindfolded and stands at one side of the
room.
(2) His partner encourages him verbally to walk, and then run
across the room towards him where he will catch him safely
in the 'safety-net' of his arms.
(3) The partners reverse roles.

## Game Eighteen — *trust*

(1) Group members stand, shoulder to shoulder, in a close
circle.
(2) One person goes into the middle of the circle and closes his
eyes.
(3) The group hold out their hands towards the person in the
centre, who sways backwards, forwards, sideways and is
firmly, but gently, supported by them.
(4) Each person has a turn at being supported by the group.

## Game Nineteen — *I have a secret*

(1) The group sits in a circle and each member thinks of something he considers to be a personal secret from the rest of
the group.
(2) In turn, each member does not disclose the secret but says
how he thinks this particular group might react were he to
tell them, e.g., with laughter, sympathy, support.

## (2) EXERCISES WHICH ENABLE THE GROUP TO WORK TOGETHER ON A TASK

Once the leader feels that members of the group trust each other and that the group has developed warmth and a fair degree of cohesion, he can introduce games and exercises which will explore how a group tackles a group task, deals with individuals and solves problems.

### Game Twenty – number problem

(1) If there are, for example, ten members in the group, excluding the leader, a set of cards is made containing ten cards of each number from one to ten.

(2) Each member is given a set of ten cards from one to ten.

(3) The leader defines the task by stating that the object of the game is for each member of the group to finish up with ten cards of one particular number.

Groups will solve this problem and complete the task in different ways which will be discussed at the end of the exercises, e.g., one group may interpret the exercise as an individual competition; another group may throw up a leader who directs the group to make ten piles of cards, each pile containing one number and then each person is given one set of numbers.

### Game Twenty-one – jigsaw problem

(1) Assuming again that there are ten children in the group, the leader makes a jigsaw by cutting a large piece of white paper into ten irregular pieces, see *Figure 7(1)*.

*Figure 7(1)* Jig-saw problem

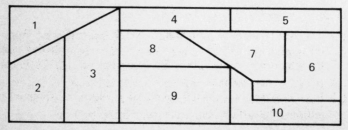

(2) The leader keeps a key copy of the jigsaw and gives the other ten pieces to the group — one piece for each person.

(3) The group is told to see how quickly it can complete the jigsaw.

Once again this exercise will reveal those with leadership potential and other roles in the group which can be discussed at the end of the exercise.

## Game Twenty-two — clay island

(1) If the group is large, divide the children into small groups of three or four.

(2) Give each group some clay, twigs, leaves, etc., and ask them to make an island.

(3) When the island is made each child chooses a personal territory and marks this out.

(4) Each group elects a leader who then gives different responsibilities to each member of the group.

## Game Twenty-three — Lego model

(1) Before the group meeting the leader constructs a fairly complex model out of Lego building materials.

(2) The group is given a set length of time in which, with another set of Lego, to copy the model.

(3) When the exercise is completed the leader asks the group to discuss how the group did or didn't work as a team — was a leader elected? Did all members participate? Was one member scape goated?

## Game Twenty-four — group story

(1) The group sits in a circle.

(2) The leader gives the opening line of a story, e.g. 'John decided that, as it was a sunny day, he would take his dog into the woods and explore. He was just entering the wood when suddenly he saw. . . .

(3) In turn, going round the circle, each member adds a line or two to the story.

*Game Twenty-five – group decision making*

(1) The leader explains that he is giving the group an exercise to see how well they can make joint decisions and arrive at a consensus of opinion.

(2) He specifies the length of time to be given to complete the task, e.g. half an hour.

(3) He gives them a sheet as follows:

'INSTRUCTIONS: You are a member of a space crew originally scheduled to rendezvous with a mother ship on the lighted surface of the moon. Due to mechanical difficulties, however, your ship was forced to land at a spot some 200 miles from the rendezvous point. During landing, much of the equipment aboard was damaged, and, since survival depends on reaching the mother ship, the most critical items available must be chosen for the 200-mile trip. Below are listed the 15 items left intact and undamaged after landing. Your task is to rank order them in terms of their importance to your crew in allowing them to reach the rendezvous point. Place the number 1 by the most important item, the number 2 by the second most important, and so on, through number 15, the least important. You have 15 minutes to complete the exercise.

_____ Box of matches
_____ Food concentrate
_____ 50 feet of nylon rope
_____ Parachute silk
_____ Portable heating unit
_____ Two .45 calibre pistols
_____ One case dehydrated Pet milk
_____ Two 100-lb tanks of oxygen
_____ Stellar map (of the moon's constellation)
_____ Life raft
_____ Magnetic compass
_____ 5 gallons of water
_____ Signal flares
_____ First aid kit containing injection needles
_____ Solar-powered FM receiver-transmitter'

*Game Twenty-six – lifeboat*

(1) The leader makes a set of cards to equal the number in the group. On each card he puts the name of a well-known job or profession, e.g. Banker, Policeman, Teacher, Comedian, Poacher, Judge, Fishmonger, Opera Singer, etc.

(2) Each member picks a card without seeing what is written on it.

(3) The leader then explains that they have all been ship-wrecked and at that moment are in the only lifeboat. The problem is that there is one person too many for the lifeboat and it is slowly sinking. The group must decide to throw one person overboard for the sake of the others.

(4) Each member of the group has two minutes to tell the group why the profession on the card he holds should qualify that person to stay in the boat.

(5) A vote is taken as to who should be thrown out.

(3) EXERCISES IN COMMUNICATION – VERBAL AND WRITTEN

Games in this category are used to show how verbal and written communication can either convey a message between two or more people accurately and effectively or can lead to inaccuracy, frustration, and anger. The ability to listen is seen to be as important as the ability to speak.

**Verbal games**

*Game Twenty-seven – word wizard*

(1) The leader says that he is a word wizard who is going to take all but four words away from each member of the group.

(2) Each member chooses and discloses the four words he wishes to keep.

(3) He goes round the circle saying them to people and listening to their words, then chooses a partner.

(4) The partnership now uses its eight words to speak to other

partnerships and eventually choose another pair giving the four people sixteen words with which to communicate.

## Game Twenty-eight — *boaster*

(1) Each person goes round the other members of the group and tells them, in a very loud voice, his own virtues and good qualities.

(2) Nobody listens because they are too busy telling everyone about their own good qualities!

(3) At the end of the exercise the group discusses the frustration experienced when people don't listen.

## Game Twenty-nine — *pass the buck*

(1) The leader provides a soft ball or something that can easily be thrown and caught.

(2) He throws it to one person who then has to talk about anything at all for two minutes.

(3) The person who has the 'Buck' then throws it to someone else who must catch it and talk for two minutes.

(4) The buck is passed between people until everyone has talked.

## Game Thirty — *sentence completion*

(1) The group sits in a circle and in turn briefly completes sentences supplied by the leader, e.g.:
   (a) Now I am thinking....
   (b) Now I am feeling....
   (c) As a baby I was....
   (d) Girls should....
   (e) Boys should....
   (f) Marriage is like....

## Game Thirty-one — *persuasion*

(1) The group appoints two people to act as judges.

(2) In turn, each member of the group comes up to the judges and tries to persuade them that he is the person to whom the one bar of chocolate should be given.

(3) The judges reach a decision and award the chocolate.

*Game Thirty-two — rumour clinic*

(1) The leader selects six members from the group to be the participants.

(2) Five of the six participants are asked to go into the isolation room. One will remain with the leader.

(3) The leader starts the tape recorder if he plans to replay the rumour clinic after the process is completed for clues to distortion.

(4) The leader reads the message to the first participant.

(5) The leader asks the second participant to return to the room.

(6) The first participant repeats what he heard from the leader to the second participant. It is important to keep in mind that each participant is to transmit the message in his own way, without help from other participants or observers.

(7) The third participant is asked to return, and the second participant repeats what he heard from the first participant.

(8) The process is repeated until all but the sixth participant has had the message transmitted to him.

(9) When the sixth participant returns to the room, he becomes the policeman. The fifth participant repeats the message to the policeman, and he in turn writes the message on the blackboard or on newsprint so that the entire group can read it.

(10) The leader then writes the original message, and it is compared with the policeman's message.

(11) The leader leads a short discussion with the entire group on the implications of the rumour clinic experience, utilizing the tape recorder if the rumour clinic has been taped. Observers may be asked to report, followed by reactions of participants.

The message to be read to the first participant could be something like the following:

*Accident report*

'I cannot wait to report to the police what I saw in this accident. It is imperative that I get to the hospital as soon as

*Figure 7(2)* Two-way communication

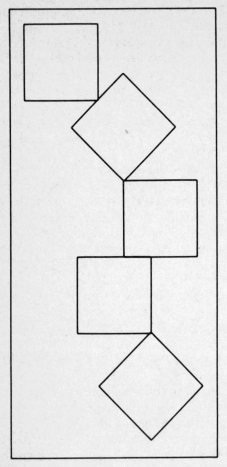

possible. The semi truck, heading south, was turning right at the intersection when the sports car, heading north, attempted to turn left. When they saw that they were turning into the same lane, they both honked their horns but proceeded to turn without slowing down. In fact, the sports car seemed to be accelerating just before the crash.'

*Figure 7(3)* One-way communication

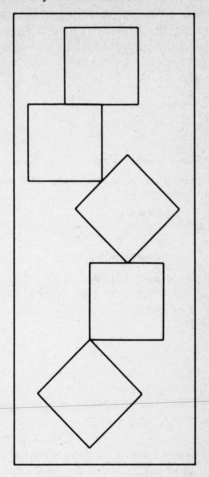

*Game Thirty-three − two-way communication*

*Instructions:* Study *Figure 7(2)*. Facing the group, you are to instruct the participants how to draw them. Begin with the top square and describe each in succession, taking particular note of the relationship of each to the proceeding one. Answer all the questions from participants and repeat if necessary.

*Game Thirty-four  −  one-way communication*

*Instructions:* Study *Figure 7(3)*. With your back to the group, you are to instruct the participants how to draw them. Begin with the top square and describe each in succession, taking particular note of the relationship of each to the preceding one. No questions are allowed.

**Written games**

*Game Thirty-five  −  coat of arms*

(1) Give each person a large sheet of paper and several coloured felt-tip pens.
(2) Ask them to design a coat of arms on the model shown in *Figure 7(4)*.

*Game Thirty-six  −  advertisement*

(1) Give each person a sheet of lined paper and ask him to write out four advertisements designed to sell himself as:
    (a) a son or daughter;
    (b) a friend;
    (c) a pupil;
    (d) a boyfriend or girlfriend.
(2) Ask each member to read out his advertisements and get the group to vote on which one would make them buy.

*Game Thirty-seven  −  characteristics*

(1) In turn, one member of the group goes out of the room with a pen and paper and writes down six characteristics which he feels describe him, e.g. moody, good sense of humour, ugly, generous, sporty, selfish.
(2) Meanwhile the leader has been collecting, on a blackboard, characteristics of the person outside the room from each remaining member of the group.
(3) The person comes back into the room and reads out his own list which is compared with the list on the blackboard and discussed.

*Figure 7(4)* Coat of arms

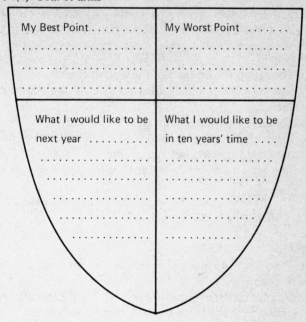

| My Best Point . . . . . . . . . <br> . . . . . . . . . . . . . . . . . . . <br> . . . . . . . . . . . . . . . . . . . <br> . . . . . . . . . . . . . . . . . . . | My Worst Point . . . . . . . <br> . . . . . . . . . . . . . . . . . . . <br> . . . . . . . . . . . . . . . . . . . <br> . . . . . . . . . . . . . . . . . . . |

What I would like to be next year . . . . . . . . . .

What I would like to be in ten years' time . . . .

## (4) EXERCISES IN COMMUNICATION – NON-VERBAL

All the encounter therapists stress the importance of non-verbal communication in our relationships with other people. Books, such as *Body Language* (Fast 1970) have made a detailed and interesting study of the subject. The following exercises are designed to help the children in the group to be aware of their non-verbal communication.

*Game Thirty-eight – mime box*

(1) The group sits in a close circle and the leader explains that an imaginary box is going to be passed round the circle. Each person will pretend to take something out of the box and mime what it is for the rest of the group, having started by miming the size of the box.

(2) When the group has guessed what is being mimed, that person hands the box on to the person on his right who then

mimes the size of his box and the object he has taken out of it, e.g. a watch, a new car, a piano, a ring, and so on round the group.

## Game Thirty-nine – blind recognition

(1) The group sits on the floor in a tight circle.
(2) One member is blindfolded and sits in the centre of the circle.
(3) The leader points at a member of the group who kneels in front of the 'blind' person who is allowed to feel the face only of the person in front of him.
(4) The person who is blindfolded has to guess whose face he is feeling.
(5) This can be varied by presenting someone's hands instead of their face to be recognized.

## Game Forty – pounce

(1) The group sits in a circle and one person is chosen to start the game.
(2) He goes up to anyone in the group and either touches him or pulls a face at him in any way that he feels like.
(3) He sits down and that person comes and does to him what he has just done, then goes on to make a different gesture to another member of the group, who in turn repeats it back, then goes on to someone else.
(4) The principle of 'do as you would be done by' is discussed.

## Game Forty-one – computer

(1) The group sits in a circle and one person volunteers to be the first 'Computer'.
(2) He stands in front of anyone in the circle who then has to ask him a question in the form of 'Stand in front of the person who. . . .' (This can be anything from, e.g., 'you would like to go on holiday with' to 'the unhappiest person in the room'.)
(3) The 'Computer' answers the question by standing in front of the person he feels is the answer.
(4) That person then gives him another question.

(5) When he has answered three questions he changes places with the last 'answer' who then becomes the new 'Computer'.

## Game Forty-two — inclusion/exclusion

(1) The group forms a tight, standing circle and one person who is inside tries to break out of the circle.
(2) Another person who is outside the circle tries to break in.
(3) The group tries to prevent either happening.

## Game Forty-three — chain mime

(1) Rather like the game of Chinese Whispers, when a phrase is whispered in turn round the circle and is usually totally distorted by the time it reaches the last person, this game uses mime.
(2) One person mimes an activity, e.g. changing a baby's nappy; the next person copies his mime and so on until it reaches the last person.
(3) The first person then reveals what his mime was.

## Game Forty-four — buddha

(1) The group divides into pairs who sit opposite each other and maintain eye-contact throughout the game.
(2) The leader asks a number of questions which each partner answers to himself — non-verbally, e.g.:
Look into your partner's eyes;
Is he an ambitious person?
Does he like reading?
Has he got a good sense of humour?
What animal does he remind you of?
What is his favourite colour?
How well do you feel you understand your partner?
(3) Partners then discuss their answers with each other.

## Game Forty-five — make way for me

(1) Two members of the group stand opposite each other, palms of hands pressed tightly together, and standing as far away from each other as possible.

(2) Another person joins in and the circle has to widen.

(3) This continues until the whole group is included.

## Game Forty-six — rock the baby

(1) Each person in turn is held in the air by the entire group and is 'rocked like a baby'.

(2) Group members say how they felt during this experience.

### (5) INCREASING THE AWARENESS CONTINUUM — PHYSICAL

The following exercises are designed to help the members of the group to be more aware of their physical senses and sensations and to sharpen up perception:

## Game Forty-seven — awareness of self and surroundings

(1) Deep breathing: lie on the floor, eyes closed. Breathe as deeply as you can, attending to the effects of increased oxygen intake. Fantasize observing your breathing from the inside.

(2) Feeling hands: with your right hand feel your left hand. Be aware of touching yourself. Then reverse, exploring your right hand.

(3) Pressure points: mentally check over your entire body and locate all of the pressure points (your bottom, your shoes, your bra strap, your belt, etc.).

(4) Washing hands: wash your hands with sand, salt, snow, or an ice cube. Pay close attention to all of the feelings you experience.

(5) Eating bread: eat a piece of bread, freely associating on the subject of bread while being aware of taste, texture, etc.

(6) Stretching: extend your left arm as high above your head as you can. Then extend your right arm. Stand as high on your tiptoes as you can. Then try to take up as much space as you can.

(7) Tapping and slapping: with your fingertips lightly tap all over your head (or a partner's head), feeling the effects of the touch. Then slap as many areas of your body as you can.

*Game Forty-eight − lemons*

(1) The group sits in a circle and the leader gives each person a lemon, explaining that no two lemons are ever exactly the same.

(2) Each person has a few minutes to 'get acquainted' with his lemon.

(3) The lemons are all placed in a pile in the centre, then redistributed.

(4) Group members pass the lemons round from left to right until they feel they are touching 'their lemon' which they keep.

*Game Forty-nine − mirror image*

(1) The group divides into pairs who stand facing each other.

(2) In turn, partners are the Mirror and the Image − whatever actions and gestures the Mirror person makes the Image person has to copy exactly.

*Game Fifty − human machines*

(1) The group first works in pairs to use their bodies to design a human machine with moving parts, e.g. a lawn mower.

(2) Pairs join together to make a machine using four bodies.

(3) Four double up and so on until the whole group is making one machine.

(6) INCREASING THE AWARENESS CONTINUUM − EMOTIONALLY

Once members of the group have built up a sense of trust and security in the group through some of the exercises described above, they will feel free to explore and express their emotions and sensations in an uninhibited way. The following games are designed to explore this expansion of feeling.

*Game Fifty-one − space stretch*

(1) Each person lies on the floor and closes his eyes.

(2) With his hands, he explores the space which he occupies and tries to 'stretch his space'.

### Game Fifty-two − *now I am aware*

(1) Each person lies on the floor with eyes closed.
(2) He listens to all the sounds which are right outside the room.
(3) He then concentrates on listening to all the sounds inside the room.
(4) Finally, he concentrates on the sounds which are going on within himself.
(5) This game can be extended to include what he can smell and taste.

### Game Fifty-three − *silence is fragile*

(1) The group is asked to sit for two minutes in absolute silence and think of a sound which would shatter the silence.
(2) The leader goes round the circle touching people at random.
(3) When he touches a person that person makes his sound and shatters the silence.

### Game Fifty-four − *pillow pounding*

(1) Each person is given a cushion or pillow.
(2) He is told to pound the pillow vigorously, making any noises which come into his head.
(3) He then hugs the pillow in an affectionate way.

### Game Fifty-five − *yell*

(1) The members of the group, at a given signal from the leader, yell as loudly as possible any of the following: his name, how he feels, a nonsense word, the name of someone he loves or hates, a taboo word.
(2) The leader claps his hands after which silence is maintained for one minute.

### Game Fifty-six − *group yell*

(1) The group crouch in a circle and the leader starts to hum quietly.
(2) Going round the circle anti-clockwise, each member joins in the humming.

(3) When the whole group is humming the leader gives a hand signal and the whole group jumps up and gives a huge yell.

### Game Fifty-seven − birth trauma

(1) The children are asked to lie on the floor and, with their eyes closed, to curl up in the foetal position.
(2) They are then asked to imagine that they are about to be born and are struggling into the outside world.
(3) When each child feels that his moment of birth has come he quickly stands up, stretches his whole body, and screams.

#### (7) UNFINISHED BUSINESS

Encounter group therapy run on a gestalt model has, as its focus, the 'unfinished business' of unresolved feelings from the group member's earlier life. These feelings are brought out into the open and dealt with in the 'here and now' in an atmosphere of confrontation backed up by group emotional support. The following exercises illustrate some of the ways in which group members can start to explore their 'unfinished business':

### Game Fifty-eight − fear in a hat

(1) The group sit in a circle and each member has paper and a pen.
(2) Each member writes down first his biggest fear, then on another piece of paper his greatest wish.
(3) These are placed in two hats which the leader then passes round the circle and each member draws out one 'fear' and one 'wish'.
(4) In turn, these are read to the group who try (a) to identify who wrote it and (b) to suggest ways of overcoming the fear and gaining the wish.

### Game Fifty-nine − top dog, under-dog

(1) The therapist explains Perls' concept of top dog and under dog (see p. 173), i.e. the top dog represents the controlling part of our personality, based on what we have been told we should do; the under-dog is the helpless, apologetic part of

our personality which submits without protest to external control. Neither represents our true self.

(2) Each member makes his right hand into his top dog and his left hand his under-dog and the two hands hold a conversation with each other.

(3) Members of the group use their two hands to hold conversations with other people in the group, e.g. top dog to top dog or one person's top dog to another person's under-dog. The top dog hand uses a very high voice and the under-dog hand a very low voice.

## Game Sixty – *unfinished conversation*

(1) The group sits in a circle in which there is one empty chair.

(2) Volunteers from the group, in turn, place an imaginary person in the chair, e.g. mother, father, baby brother, and has a minute to say to that person some of the things he would like, but has never dared, to say to him or her, e.g. 'I have placed my father in the chair; I say to him – Why did you always seem to love my sister more than me? Why?'

## Game Sixty-one – *gripes auction*

(1) Each person is told that he has 100 points which he can use to bid for gripes, i.e. complaints from the following list:
teachers
parents
school
the residential community
social workers
sisters and brothers
doctors
police
houseparents.

(2) The leader puts each possible gripe up for auction in turn and group members use their 100 points to bid for and buy their favourite gripe.

## Game Sixty-two – *you remind me of. . . .*

(1) The group divides into pairs who sit opposite each other and take turns at being the speaker and the listener.

(2) The speaker looks and thinks about his partner and then says of whom that person reminds him. He then goes on to say:
   (a) what it is that is the same about the two people,
   (b) what he would like to say to that person if he were there,
   (c) how the person present is different from the one with whom he is likened.

*Game Sixty-three − unfinished business*

(1) The group divides into pairs who sit opposite each other and reverse roles half-way through the exercise.
(2) Each person puts himself in the role of his parent of the opposite sex and spends two minutes, in that role, talking to his partner about himself as the son or daughter of the imagined parent, describing strengths, weaknesses, and conflicts between the parent and child which are still un-resolved.

(8) GAMES TO INCREASE CREATIVITY AND
SPONTANEITY, TO EXPLORE FANTASY AND TO
HAVE FUN

An important goal in encounter group therapy is to help the members of the group to realize their potential for being creative and for letting their imaginations take over as a way of getting into touch with their feelings and fantasies. There are many ways of encouraging this process in a group therapy meeting and some of the exercises following will be included in most encounter groups.

*Game Sixty-four − using paper, charcoal, and paints*
The following suggestions bring the use of art into the group session.

(a) In pairs or groups of four a joint picture is painted without the use of any verbal communication between the artists.
(b) The leader starts a drawing in chalk on a blackboard, group members in turn come up to the board and add something to the picture or rub something out.

(c) A large piece of paper is divided into the same number of squares as there are people in the group. Each person in turn draws something in a square which depicts something about his life either at home or in the residential community.

(d) With a good supply of magazines, scissors, and glue the group constructs a collage which represents life in their residential community.

(e) Partners take turns in drawing full-sized silhouettes of each other. Silhouettes are then hung on the wall, the name of the person is added, and group members move from silhouette to silhouette adding the features they associate with that person.

## Game Sixty-five — magic drum

(1) Members of the group take turns in beating a drum and the group moves to the beat of the drum.

(2) The drummer shouts out an adjective which describes the beat and the group acts out that adjective in movement, e.g. old, young, jerky, smooth.

## Game Sixty-six — true or false?

(1) Two people go out of the room and each thinks of an interesting incident in their earlier childhood to recount to the group — one story is true, the other is pure fantasy.

(2) The two people come back into the room and each tells his story.

(3) The group has to decide which story is fact and which story is fantasy.

## Game Sixty-seven — group fantasies

Fantasies created by the group can be made with the whole group taking part or with only sub-groups. Three major variations are common.

(A) Everyone sits in a circle with their eyes closed. Someone begins a fantasy involving the entire group. Group members contribute to the story as they feel a part of it.

(B) One member lies on the floor and begins a fantasy. Other participants are free to join him on the floor and become a part of the dream and contribute to it, and individual participants may leave the fantasy by getting up from the floor.

(C) All of the participants of the group lie on the floor with their heads together, their bodies forming the spokes of a wheel. In this way, whispers can be heard by everyone. Someone begins a fantasy, either alone or involving one or more other group participants, and others contribute as they identify with the story.

Any group participant should feel free to suggest that the fantasy be terminated. Later discussion might centre around such dimensions as the fantasy content, group cohesiveness, tensions and sub-groupings within the group, feelings experienced during the exercise, roles participants played in the story, etc.

*Game Sixty-eight – guided group fantasy*

(1) The leader invites the group to participate in an exploratory trip. He asks them to make themselves as comfortable as possible and to close their eyes.

(2) He explains that he will tell them what is happening on the trip and that they are to listen and fantasize their surroundings and experiences. He tells them that from time to time he will ask them questions. They are to answer these in their own minds, and they will be asked to answer them openly in the group when the experience is over.

(3) The following script should be read slowly in a non-abrasive tone of voice:[1]

'We have all gathered together to go down the Colorado River on a raft. We will be led by competent guides, but it will be rough. You must be prepared for a number of critical situations. It will be exciting and pleasurable, but at times it might be painful and dangerous. Contemplate this, consider it, and decide whether you want to go along. If you have some resistance, is there anyone in the group that convinces you to go? How does he or she do it? Do you convince

[1] This script is reprinted from: J. William Pfeiffer and John E. Jones (eds) A Handbook of Structured Experiences for Human Relations Training. San Diego, CA: University Associates, 1973. Used with permission.

someone else who is reluctant? How do you do it? Whom do you particularly want to go with you on this trip?

'We gather in the boat, our guide at the helm. It is a beautiful day as we start down the river; it is calm and peaceful. In the warm sun, the boat smoothly moving through the waters, you find your mind wandering off. Catch the thought. What are you thinking about? What are you feeling? What reveries do you engage in?

'The boat moves faster, and you see white waters ahead. You are a bit apprehensive, but soon you are in amidst the current. The raft is gently tossed about, but you come through smoothly and easily. This is your first taste of shooting the rapids. As you move down the river, with the cliffs becoming taller and taller on either side of the bank, you find the river moving faster and faster − the white waters becoming more turbulent. You learn that the rapids are rated on a scale from one to ten, and those that you have just gone through are rated two to three. They increase in force, and you are going through rapids rated six and seven. The raft is tossed about, but you cling, getting the excitement and the full taste of the thrill of the waters splashing around you − turning and twisting the raft. You come to a bend in the river, and your guide tells you that the next rapid is scaled ten, but because of the bend in the river it is possible for you to land before reaching the rapids and walk across a spot of land and regain the raft on the other side. You thus have a chance to get off. Do you do so, or do you go on? Do you have a moment of fear? Does anybody convince you to stay on? How? Do you convince anybody else to stay on? How?

'You do go on. The raft is tossed, sometimes tilting at a forty-five degree angle. It turns so that you are going down backwards, then hits a rock and spins around again. Catch the feeling of the turmoil and note your feelings. The twisting and turning diminish. You are out of it and now are moving smoothly and quietly down the waters. What are you feeling?

'Your guide tells you it is time now to rest and seek new

adventures, and he lands the raft at the mouth of a blind canyon. He tells you that you will be there for a few hours and that you can explore the canyon. You move into it and find the tall cliffs on either side getting narrower and narrower above you until you are in the middle of a tunnel. It becomes darker and darker. What do you feel? You push on into the blackness, seeing no light behind you or ahead. Do you have any fears? What do you fear?

'Suddenly light shines ahead, and you find yourself at the mouth of a large cave, which is well lighted. The cave is guarded by a gatekeeper, who informs you that there is a treasure within. Each of you has to supply a ticket of admission – something of yourself which you will give in order to enter the cave. Stop now, open your eyes, and with the material supplied make a ticket, giving something of yourself so that you can proceed.'

(4) The leader distributes the art materials and allows the participants to draw, write, or in some way construct their 'ticket'.

(5) He continues the fantasy:

'You offer your ticket to the gatekeeper and enter the treasure room. What is your treasure?

'You enjoy your treasure, and then the gatekeeper tells you that you must go on, leaving the treasure behind. What do you feel? You pass out of the cave through a short tunnel and find yourself back on the beach, where your raft has been anchored. With surprise you look behind you and cannot see the crevice out of which you came. The cave is lost. How do you feel?

'Night has now fallen. You see the sky above you up through the canyon; the stars are bright, and a warm breeze engulfs you. The river is flowing swiftly and quietly. You sit around a campfire, reflecting on your adventure, and you think back on all that took place during the day. What does it all mean to you?

'We are now back to today. Here we are in this room. Let us review the answers in your mind.'

(6) The leader asks various members the answers to each of the

questions posed during the fantasy. When he reaches the subject of the ticket of admission, he asks participants to show, discuss, and interact with others concerning what they gave of themselves. The leader continues until all of the questions have been dealt with and ends by assisting the group in talking through the impact of the experience.

(9) ROLE PLAY AND PSYCHODRAMA

To develop empathy for, and an understanding of, other people's feelings and attitudes as well as one's own is a valuable part of coming to terms with reality and learning to adjust to life as it is as opposed to life as we would like it to be. Role play exercises and psychodrama are techniques which can be used in an encounter group therapy session to develop these skills.

*Game Sixty-nine − newspaper heading*

(1) The group is divided into three small groups and each group is given a headline cut from a newspaper which evokes a family crisis.

(2) Each group makes up a short sketch based on the heading which it acts for the other groups.

*Game Seventy − sculpture*

(1) The group chooses an incident which has happened in the residential community in the previous week and has caused trouble, e.g. two children were caught stealing something from another child who became very violent with them when he discovered the theft.

(2) One person in the group volunteers to make a sculpture depicting this scene using members of the group to depict each person in the tableau.

(3) Another member of the group rearranges the sculpture to show how relationships would have been had this theft not taken place.

*Game Seventy-one − puppets*

(1) Puppets depicting members of a family are bought or made.

(2) Half the group produces a puppet play for the rest of the group based on something which has happened in a family with whom they are familiar.

(3) The audience criticizes the production, then offers solutions for 'happy endings' to the play.

*Game Seventy-two — group sculpture*

(1) One person volunteers to arrange another person as a sculpture.

(2) A second person then joins the first sculptor onto his sculpture and this continues until the entire group has formed one giant sculpture.

*Game Seventy-three — pantomimes*

(1) The group is divided into fours and each four is given a set of 'props' which might include a hat, a wig, a walking stick, a gun, etc.

(2) Each group invents a story which incorporates the props and acts it for the other groups. One person acts as the narrator and sound-effects person, the other three act.

*Game Seventy-four — role play generally*

Any situation arising in the daily life of the residential community which causes problems in relationships or organization can be role played with the protagonists from the real-life situation playing different roles from their own reality roles.

This role play can be extended to include situations from a child's family background should a child express a desire to deal with his problem in this way.

(10) FEEDBACK – POSITIVE AND NEGATIVE

Perhaps the most important feature of encounter group therapy is the feedback about self which the group sessions provide. This feedback will not always be positive and it is vital for the group leader to be able to use negative feedback, not as a means of destroying a person but as a means of helping him towards a better acceptance of himself. One of the criticisms of confronting group therapy is that it can destroy someone's defences before he has any real ego strength to put in their place. Feedback games and exercises are of immense value, provided that there is adequate emotional support and security in the group for those members receiving the feedback.

*Game Seventy-five — gossip*

(1) Members of the group take it in turn to go out of the room.
(2) Two of the remaining members of the group each make a statement about the person who is out: (a) something they like very much about the person; (b) something they would like him to change about himself.
(3) The person re-enters the room and is asked which he would like first — the good news or the bad news.
(4) The two statements are read out to him and he tries to guess who made them.

*Game Seventy-six — family cards*

(1) The leader produces a set of cards on which the roles of family members are written, i.e. mother, father, son, daughter, brother, sister, grandfather, grandmother, husband, wife.
(2) In turn, members of the group give these cards out to individuals in the group who might represent that role for them.
(3) People discuss how they felt when given certain cards.

*Game Seventy-seven — adjective cards*

(1) As a variation on the previous game, the leader gives out cards with different adjectives written on them, e.g. stormy, hot, cold, opaque, steel, hard, soft.
(2) Members of the group give these cards out to each other as a comment on their perception of each person.

*Game Seventy-eight — pecking order*

(1) Ask the group to arrange itself in a line starting with the most influential and powerful member of the group at the front down to the least influential member at the end of the line.

(2) Discuss how to cope with stress and feedback, especially if it is negative.

*Game Seventy-nine – feedback*

(1) The group sits in a circle in which there is one empty chair – the 'hot seat'.
(2) In turn, each member of the group sits in the hot seat and the other members each make two statements to him beginning (a) I dislike you because. . . . (b) I like you because.
. . .

*Game Eighty – mail box*

(1) Each member of the group takes off a shoe which he puts in front of him.
(2) Each member of the group writes a positive comment on a piece of card about each of the other members and then 'posts it' into his shoe which is the mail box.
(3) The postman empties the mail box and reads out the cards.

SUMMARY

In this chapter some of the games and exercises it is possible to use when running an encounter group therapy session have been discussed under broad categories which describe the major aim of the games. These are intended to give an introduction to the use of games and the residential group worker would be able to adapt and develop them to suit his particular group. They may also serve as a stimulus for the invention of further games and encourage the residential therapist to build up his own repertoire of encounter games and exercises.

# 8 Conclusion

On re-reading the preface to this book, I realize that my original aim of presenting three major personality theories and the forms of therapy which arose from them in a simple, easily digestible form was perhaps over-ambitious! Theoretical knowledge and practical experience which have been accumulated over twenty-five years acquire a certain patina of facile simplicity which belies the personal and professional growing pains and feelings of inadequacy and failure which every residential therapist experiences throughout his professional development. The moments of reward, however, are very real. I hope I have conveyed this, to some degree, to young residential therapists who are perhaps still coming to terms with the fact that, whereas we are not omnipotent and cannot be all things to all children we can, nevertheless, develop professional skills which will help at least some children to come to terms with some of their problems.

In presenting three distinctly differing group therapies, the accent has been on the emphasis which each therapy places on feelings, thought processes, and behaviours. The residential therapist, however, cannot afford the luxury of concentrating solely on any one of these aspects when living and working within a residential community as he is intimately and almost continuously involved with caring for and helping 'the whole child' who thinks, feels, and behaves simultaneously.

Theories which are evolved to underpin a set of practical skills are not as neat or as watertight as I may have made them appear in my effort to condense concepts which people have spent a lifetime in conceptualizing. At any given moment a residential therapist may be drawing, often intuitively, on a cross-section of ideas and experiences drawn from sources as varied as books, experiences they remember from their own upbringing and education, and unconscious modelling on colleagues with more experience.

Formal training and the absorption of theory can never replace the natural instinct, sensitivity, and intuitive therapeutic approach with which the best residential therapists are armed. Like Moliére's 'Bourgeois Gentilhomme', who was delighted to discover that he had been speaking 'prose' all his life, the effective residential therapist, when he delves into the theories of his profession, will often find that he has been talking 'therapy' all his life!

Where I do feel that the knowledge of theoretical concepts of group therapy can be of value to the residential worker is in helping him:

(a) To start to be able to understand himself well enough to acknowledge his own strengths and weaknesses which will, in turn, help him to choose the particular method of therapy at which he is likely to be most successful at that stage of his career.

(b) To open his mind to the possibility of there being more than one way in which to assess and define a child's problems and more than one way in which to offer successful treatment.

(c) To develop his own self-confidence and self-esteem by discovering that there is no 'magical' set of answers possessed solely by people with degrees in psychology or psychiatry and that the arguments which take place between opposing schools of thought only serve to prove this point!

(d) To be stimulated to try something new — to run an encounter group or to introduce a simple form of behaviour modification or to start a Warm Fuzzy campaign.

I fully realize that, as head of a residential community, I am in a much easier position to introduce new ideas and experiments than someone in a junior position but I am also aware that some of the most exciting ideas, the use of a token economy springs to mind, have been introduced to my community by other members of staff. If one is introducing a new form of group therapy, it is often more feasible to start in a small way and build up gradually to a complete treatment method, enlisting the enthusiasm of colleagues along the way. Some staff, even those in charge of residential establishments, can all too readily adopt a defeatist attitude to the introduction of any change or new idea on the basis that 'they', the 'system', the 'establishment' will not allow changes to take place. In T.A. terms they have put themselves into a victim role and whenever some exciting change is suggested, however minor, they will play the 'Yes, but, . . .' game! From personal experience of working at all levels within a residential community and from within both social services and educational authorities, I firmly believe that if one has the courage of one's convictions, an ability to admit when one is wrong, and the urge to create a dynamic institution, then new methods and ways of looking at our work can be introduced successfully, if only from very small beginnings.

One of the fears sometimes expressed by residential workers about the learning of theories is that they will lose their 'spontaneity' and natural ability to make easy relationships with children by becoming more conscious of the mechanics of their trade. The process of learning new skills in residential care is exactly like that experienced by anyone attempting to improve professional skills. A 'natural' batsman may at first feel hampered by a coach who forces him to study and rehearse his different strokes but the techniques he is taught will gradually be absorbed into his 'natural' game and his feeling of spontaneity will return, enhanced by the confidence given to him by having learnt from someone with more experience.

Although I have tended to go through stages of enthusiasm for one particular theoretical approach, I now firmly believe that, at one level, the particular theory of the moment, the 'flavour of the month', is not only unimportant but is almost irrelevant compared with the basic underlying philosophy which supports the whole superstructure of a residential community.

My own philosophy of residential care has changed very little over the years and I feel it has much in common with a wide variety of residential establishments which are as different in organizational structure and character as the people who run them. Some of the essentials of this philosophy are self-respect and respect for others; a belief in the value of one's work combined with a realistic lack of omnipotence, which can only lead to non-productive feelings of inadequacy; a desire to develop, through understanding, a genuine acceptance and tolerance of others while providing opportunities for personal growth and self-actualization for staff and children alike, and a sense of fun as well as a seriousness of purpose.

For anyone who may have been stimulated in some small way to attempt some of the group therapy ideas suggested in this book, I have included, in the appendix, some suggestions for further reading and organizations which may offer practical help and inspiration.

# Appendix

(1) For people interested in reading more about the theory and practice of transactional analysis the following books may be helpful:

Berne, E. (1961) *Transactional Analysis in Psychotherapy*. New York: Grove Press.

_____ (1964) *Games People Play*. New York: Grove Press.

_____ (1966) *Principles of Group Treatment*. New York: Oxford University Press.

_____ (1972) *What do you say after you say Hello?* New York: Grove Press.

Harris, T. A. (1969) *I'm O.K. – You're O.K.* New York: Harper & Row.

James, M. and Jongeward, D. (1971) *Born to Win*. Reading, Mass.: Addison-Wesley.

_____ (1975) *The People Book*. Menlo Park, CA: Addison-Wesley.

Woollams, S. and Brown, M. (1979) *The Total Handbook of Transactional Analysis*. Englewood Cliffs, N.J.: Prentice-Hall.

(2) For people interested in reading more about behaviour modification the following books may be helpful:

Chaffin, J. and Kroth, R. (1971) *Workshop on Behaviour Modification*. Indiana: Hammond.

Dollard, J. and Miller, N. E. (1950) *Personality and Psychotherapy*. New York: McGraw-Hill.

Eysenck, H. J. (ed.) (1964) *Experiments in Behaviour Therapy*. Oxford: Pergamon.

Gagne, R. M. (1965) *The Conditions of Learning*. New York: Holt, Rinehart & Winston.

Jehu, D. (1967) *Learning Theory and Social Work*. London: Routledge & Kegan Paul.

Poteet, J. A. (1974) *Behaviour Modification*. London: University of London Press.

(3) For people interested in reading more about encounter group theory and practice the following books may be helpful:

De Mille, R. (1967) *Put Your Mother on the Ceiling: Children's Imagination Games*. New York: Walker.

Fagan, J. and Shepherd, I. L. (1951) *Gestalt Theory*. Harmondsworth: Penguin Education.

Howard, J. (1970) *Please Touch*. New York: McGraw-Hill.

Lewis, H. R. and Streitfeld, H. S. (1973) *Growth Games*. London: Sphere.

Schultz, D. (1977) *Growth Psychology*. New York: Van Nostrand.

Schutz, W. C. (1967) *Joy: Expanding Human Awareness*. New York: Grove Press.

Weitz, S. (1974) *Non-Verbal Communication*. New York and London: Oxford University Press.

Several organizations run workshops on group therapy and these are usually advertised locally in newspapers, journals, and prospectuses from colleges and universities. The Association of Workers with Maladjusted Children (General Secretary John Cross), New Barns School, Church Lane, Toddington, Glos.; local branches of the professional social work associations, B.A.S.W. and R.C.A., also publish articles and run workshops in all forms of group therapy. Group workshops are often advertised nationally in the journal *New Society*.

# References

Badaines, J. and Ginzburg, M. (1979) Therapeutic Communities and the New Therapies. In R. D. Hinshelwood and N. Manning (eds) *Therapeutic Communities*. London: Routledge & Kegan Paul.

Balbernie, R. (1966) *Residential Work with Children*. Oxford: Pergamon Press.

Bales, R. F. (1958) Task Roles and Social Roles in Problem Solving Groups. In Maccoby, E. E., Newcomb, M., and Hartley, E. L. (eds) *Readings in social psychology*. 3rd edn, New York: Holt, Rinehart, & Winston.

Bandura, A. (1965). Behaviour Modification through Modeling Procedures. In L. P. Ullman and L. Krasner (eds) *Research in Behaviour Modification*. New York: Holt, Rinehart, and Winston.

Bandura, A. and MacDonald, F. J. (1963) The Influence of Social Reinforcement and the Behaviour of Models in Shaping Children's Moral Judgements. *Journal of Abnormal and Social Psychology*, **67**, 274–81.

Becker, W. C. (1971) *Parents are Teachers*. Champaign, Ill.: Research Press.

Berne, E. (1961) *Transactional Analysis in Psychotherapy*. New York: Grove Press.

____ (1964) *Games People Play*. New York: Grove Press.

____ (1974) *What Do You Say After You Say Hello?* London: André Deutsch.

Burns, T. and Stalker, G. M. (1961) *The Management of Innovation*. London: Tavistock.

Chittenden, G. E. (1942) An Experimental Study in Measuring and Modifying Assertive Behaviour in Young Children. *Monographs of the Society for Research in Child Development*, **7** (1, Serial No. 31).

Docker-Drysdale, B. (1968) *Therapy in Child Care*. London and Harlow: Longman, Green.

____ (1973) *Consultation in Child Care*. London: Longman.

Douglas, T. (1976) *Groupwork Practice*. London: Tavistock.

Ellis, A. and Harper, R. A. (1975) *A New Guide to Rational Living*. North Hollywood, California: Wilshire.

Evans, K. M. (1966) *Sociometry and Education*. London: Routledge & Kegan Paul.

Fast, J. (1970) *Body Language*. New York: M. Evans.

Freed, A. M. (1973) *T.A. for Tots*. Sacramento, California: Jalmar Press.

_____ (1976) *T.A. for Teens*. Sacramento, California: Jalmar Press.

Freed, A. M. and Freed, M. (1977) *T.A. for Kids*. (Rev. Edn). Sacramento, California: Jalmar Press.

Freud, S. (1912) 'Recommendations to Physicians Practising Psychoanalysis'. *Standard Edition of the Complete Psychological Works*, **12**, London: Hogarth.

Gittelman, M. (1965) Behavioural Rehearsal as a Technique in Child Treatment. *Journal of Child Psychology and Psychiatry*, **6**, 251–55.

Goffman, E. (1961) *Asylums*. New York: Doubleday.

Halpin, A. W. (1958) *Administrative Theory in Education*. New York: Macmillan.

Harris, F. R., Wolf, M. M., and Baer, D. M. (1964). Effects of Adult Social Reinforcement on Child Behaviour. *Young Children*, **20**, (1).

Havighurst, R. J. (1953) *Human Development and Education*. New York: Longmans.

Hey, A. (1973) Analysis and Definition of the Functions of Caring Establishments. In J. Hunter and F. Ainsworth (eds). *Residential Establishments: The Evolving of Caring Systems*. Dundee: Burns & Harris.

Hinshelwood, R. D. and Manning, N. (eds) (1979) *Therapeutic Communities*. London: Routledge & Kegan Paul.

James, M. and Jongeward, D. (1975) *The People Book*. Menlo Park, California: Addison-Wesley.

Janov, A. (1970) *The Primal Scream*. New York: Dell.

Jehu, D. (1967) *Learning Theory and Social Work*. London: Routledge & Kegan Paul.

Jones, M. (1953) *The Therapeutic Community*. New York: Basic Books.

Jones, M. C. (1924) The elimination of children's fears. *Journal of Experimental Psychology*, **7**, 383–90.

Lazarus, A. A. (1960) The Elimination of Children's Phobias by Deconditioning. In H. J. Eysenck (ed.). *Behaviour Therapy – Neuroses*. New York: Pergamon Press.

_____ (1961) Group Therapy of Phobic Disorders by Systematic Desensitization. *Journal of Abnormal and Social Psychology*, **63**, 504–10.

Lazarus, A. A. and Abramovitz, A. (1962) The Use of 'Emotive

Imagery' in the Treatment of Children's Phobias. *Journal of Mental Science*, **108**, 191–95.

Levitsky, A. and Perls, F. (1972) The Rules and Games of Gestalt Therapy. In J. Huber and L. Millman (eds), *Goals and Behaviour in Psychotherapy and Counseling*. Ohio: Merrill.

Lovaas, O. I. (1966) *Reinforcement Therapy*. (16mm. sound film). Philadelphia: Smith, Kline & French Laboratories.

Lundin, R. W. (1961) *Personality: an experimental approach*. New York: Macmillan.

Madge, C. (1951) Psychology of the environment. *Human Relations Journal*, **III**.

Maslow, A. (1968) *Toward a Psychology of Being*. New York: Van Nostrand-Reinhold.

McKenna, J. (1975) *I Feel More Like I Do Now Than When I First Came In*. St. Louis, MO: Emily Publishing and Formur, Inc.

Miller, N. E. and Dollard, J. (1941) *Social Learning and Imitation*. New Haven: Yale University Press.

Millham, A., Bullock, A., Hosie, A., and Haak, A. (1981) *Issues of Control in Residential Care*. London: HMSO.

Moreno, J. L. (1934) *Who Shall Survive? A New Approach to the Problem of Human Relations*. New York: Beacon House.

―――― (1948) *Psychodrama*. New York: Beacon House.

Napier, R. W. and Gershenfeld, M. K. (1973) *Groups: Theory and Experience*. Boston: Houghton Mifflin.

O'Connor, R. D. (1969) Modification of Social Withdrawal Through Symbolic Modeling. *Journal of Applied Behaviour Analysis*, **2**.

Osgood, C. E., Suci, J., and Tannenbaum, P. H. (1957) *The Measurement of Meaning*. Illinois: Illini.

Osmond, H. (1959) The Relationship Between Architect and Psychiatrist. In C. Goshen (ed.) *Psychiatic Architecture*. Washington: American Psychiatric Association.

Owens, R. G. (1970) *Organisational Behaviour in Schools*. Englewood Cliffs: Prentice-Hall.

Patterson, G. R. (1965) A Learning Theory Approach to the Treatment of the School Phobic Child. In L. P. Ullmann and L. Krasner (eds) *Case Studies in Behaviour Modification*. New York: Holt, Rinehart & Winston.

Pavlov, I. P. (1927) *Conditioned Reflexes*.Oxford: University Press.

Perls F. S. (1969) *Gestalt Therapy Verbatim*. Lafayette, CA.: Real People Press.

―――― (1972) *Gestalt Therapy Now*. Harmondsworth: Penguin.

―――― (1974) *Gestalt Therapy Integrated*. New York: Vintage Books.

Poteet, J. A. (1973) *Behaviour Modification. A Practical Guide for Teachers*. London: University of London Press.

Redl, F. and Wineman, D. (1952) *Controls from Within*. New York: Macmillan.

Reese, E. P. (1966) *The Analysis of Human Operant Behaviour*. Dubuque, Iowa: Brown.

Rice, A. K. (1958) *Productivity and Social Organisations: the Ahmedabad Experiment*. London: Tavistock.

—— (1961) *On Becoming a Person: A Therapist's View of Psychotherapy*. Boston: Houghton Mifflin.

—— (1970) *Carl Rogers on Encounter Groups*. New York: Harper & Row.

Rogers, C. (1951) *Client-Centred Therapy*. Boston: Houghton Mifflin.

Rose, S. D. (1973) *Treating Children in Groups*. San Francisco and London: Jossey-Bass.

Sahakian, W. S. (1965) *Psychology of Personality: Readings in Theory*. Chicago, Ill.: Rand McNally.

Schultz, D. (1977) *Growth Psychology*. New York: Van Nostrand.

Skinner, B. F. (1938) *The Behaviour of Organisms*. New York: Appleton.

—— (1953) Freedom and the control of men. In R. Ullrich and J. Mabry (eds). *Control of Human Behaviour*. Glenview, Ill.: Scott Foresman.

Steiner, C. (1974) *Scripts People Live: Transactional Analysis of Life Scripts*. New York: Grove Press.

Storr, A. (1960) *The Integrity of the Personality*. London: Heinemann.

Thompson, S. and Kahn, J. H. (1970) *The Group Process as a Helping Technique*. Oxford: Pergamon Press.

Truax, C. B. and Carkhuff, R. R. (1967) *Toward Effective Counselling and Psychotherapy*. Chicago: Aldine.

Ullmann, L. P. and Krasner, L. (eds) (1965) *Case Studies in Behaviour Modification*. New York: Holt, Rinehart & Winston.

Walters, R. H. and Llewellyn, T. E. (1963) Enhancement of Punitiveness by Visual and Audio-Visual Displays. *Canada-Journal of Psychology*, **16**, 244–55.

Watson, J. B. and Rayner, R. (1920) Conditional Emotional Reactions. *Journal of Experimental Psychology*, **3**, 1–14.

White, R. K. and Lippit, R. (1960) *Autocracy and Democracy*. New York: Harper and Row.

Winnicott, D. W. (1965) *The Maturational Process and The Facilitating Environment*. London: Hogarth Press.

Wolpe, J. (1958) *Psychotherapy by Reciprocal Inhibition*. Palo Alto, California: Stanford University Press.

Wolpe, J. and Lazarus, A. A. (1966) *Behaviour Therapy Techniques: A Guide to the Treatment of Neuroses*. Oxford: Pergamon Press.

Woollams, S. and Brown, M. (1979) *The Total Handbook of Transactional Analysis*. Englewood Cliffs, N.J.: Prentice-Hall.

# Name Index

*Figures in italics refer to bibliographical references*

# Subject Index